WITCHCRAFT:
THE OLD RELIGION

by

Dr. Leo Louis Martello

A Citadel Press Book
Published by Carol Publishing Group

First Carol Publishing Group Edition 1991

Copyright © by Dr. Leo Louis Martello

A Citadel Press Book
Published by Carol Publishing Group

Editorial Offices Sales & Distribution Offices
600 Madison Avenue 120 Enterprise Avenue
New York, NY 10022 Secaucus, NJ 07094

In Canada: Musson Book Company
A Division of General Publishing Co., Limited
Don Mills, Ontario

Citadel Press is a registered trademark of
Carol Communications, Inc.

All rights reserved. No part of this book
may be reproduced in any form, except by
a newspaper or magazine reviewer who
wishes to quote brief passages in
connection with a review.

Queries regarding rights and permissions
should be addressed to: Carol Publishing Group,
600 Madison Avenue, New York, NY 10022

Manufactured in the United States of America
ISBN 0-8065-1028-5

Carol Publishing Group books are available at special discounts
for bulk purchases, for sales promotions, fund raising, or
educational purposes. Special editions can also be created to
specifications. For details contact: Special Sales Department,
Carol Publishing Group, 120 Enterprise Ave., Secaucus, NJ 07094

12 11 10 9 8 7 6 5 4

Preface:
A Witch by Any Other Name

I am a Witch. That's capitalized the same as Catholic or Jew or Moslem. I don't believe in the Christian devil or hell or their heaven. I certainly don't worship Satan. I don't desecrate churches or graveyards, as my religion respects those who have passed on and we honor them on Halloween. I don't waste my time, thoughts, or energies on cursing people, since I know that most of them will do that for themselves without any help from me. I consider sex a sacred, private, and personal matter, so the Christian accusation of "sex orgies" is a projection of their own masturbatory fantasies—there's nothing private or personal about an orgy. I don't worship the "powers of darkness" or consider the evil principle in life as powerful. In fact I consider evil impotent. What gives it power is the support—what I call the "sanction of silence"—of the good people who don't stand up to it, those basically decent people who say nothing, do nothing, when they see evil.

I make no claims as a Witch to "supernatural powers," but I totally believe in the *super* powers that reside in the *natural*. First and foremost, as a Witch I am an Old Religionist, worshipping the pre-Christian ancient deities. They are the Horned God and the Mother Goddess, especially the latter. The coven is my church, wherever it may meet, consisting of thirteen or less Witches. All of us are priests and priestesses. In Witchcraft, the Old Religion, there is no laity as yet. Our rites and our rituals are ancient, and just as sacred to us as the rites of any other dedicated religionist. However, unlike other religions, we are all active participants in the worship, rather than passive observers. Because we all put a great deal into the worship, we all get a great deal out of it. As I wrote in the article "Who's a Witch?" in *Witchcraft Digest,* "In the final analysis a Witch is someone whose entire being is permeated with the Craft of the Wise. This is both conscious and unconscious. Such a person is constantly studying, learning, adding and eliminating things, ever seeking new knowledge, and if he or she belongs to a coven, unless physically impossible, nothing will deter his/her attendance. The covenstead is the Mecca of modern Magi, a place to replenish one's energies, recharge one's psychic batteries, renew loving relationships, identify with the Deities, experience a sense of Oneness with Congregated Crafters and Communion with the Goddess and the Horned God."

Most books written on Witchcraft are by non-Witches. They discuss Witchcraft not as it really is but as it has been defined by the Catholic and other Christian churches. Any book that states that Witches make pacts with devils, have sex orgies, or say the Lord's Prayer backwards is either blatantly deceptive or totally

Preface: A Witch by Any Other Name 13

ignorant of the truth. Any book that discusses Witches and doesn't mention the Goddess is uninformed or Christian-motivated. These books are geared to "Pop Witches" and to those who want to toy with the idea of Witchcraft as evil; their authors and readers alike titillate their own unfounded fantasies and are nothing more than renegade Judeo-Christians. Pretentious mediocrities think that it's a quick way to recognition and power. Unethical opportunists have jumped on the bandwagon, offering all kinds of mail-order "Instant Witch" courses. All of these people are unconscious agents of the big lie fostered by the Christian churches. Whether they are Bible Belt bullies, professional debunkers, believers in Beelzebub, or fast-buck artists, they all have this in common: ignorance and a lack of intellectual integrity.

A perfect example of religious bigotry and unethical reporting, based on nothing more than opinion, is the following news item, which appeared in the New York *Daily News* November, 1972, headlined "Witchcraft Is Linked to Grave Vandalism." The lead paragraph states, "The historic, 300-year-old Gravesend Cemetery in Sheepshead Bay, Brooklyn, which was saved from the oblivion of neglect during the summer by a hard-working group of youths, was heavily vandalized during the weekend, apparently by people practicing witchcraft, reported the president of the Gravesend Historical Society, Eric Ierardi.

"He said that more than a quarter of the tombstones were turned over and others were cracked. 'Some of them are irreplaceable pages of history,' he said. 'They belong to some of the first residents to settle this area.'

"Police investigating the graveyard at McDonald

Ave. and Gravesend Neck Road yesterday found about 10 dead cats, which had apparently been strangled. Their bodies were strewn about the graves, with their skulls and limbs torn off and slivers of wood piercing their heads. On one of the tombstones the vandals started a fire with hay and sticks. 'This is really a crying shame,' said the 22-year-old founder of the historical society. He said the vandalism was definitely not the work of children. 'Some of those tombstones weigh 300 pounds. It would take more than one good-sized adult to topple them.'"

This "news item" ended with the following revealing paragraph: "Ierardi said that more than 40 stones were knocked down in three long rows along with a few others scattered around the cemetery. Ierardi's group, mostly students from St. Francis College of Brooklyn and the neighborhood around the cemetery, had worked through the summer and autumn cleaning the rubble-strewn site."

Once again Witches are accused of an evil act by someone who obviously believes in the Devil, a twenty-two-year-old student from a Catholic college. When we send protest letters full of facts, they rarely are published. The rotten underbelly of yellow journalism continues to publish nonresearched "news items" linking Witches to such criminal acts.

Then there is President Nixon's bosom buddy Billy Graham, who as a spiritual leader never once spoke out against the bombings of peasants in North Vietnam, saying, "Everyone knows that there are supernatural powers in the world. Likewise, everyone would like to be in touch with these powers. But those who become involved in the occult seek these supernatural forces in astrology, in tarot card readers, in the mysteries of Eastern religions, in soothsayers, diviners of the future, psychics and seers." *Enquirer,* November 19, 1972)

Graham claims that the Bible "is the living word of God, and once a person understands it in that light, there is no need of seeking the supernatural elsewhere." To support his thesis that all forms of the occult and witchcraft are agents of the Devil, he says, "The very word witchcraft stems from the same Greek word as the word 'drugs,' and this is more than coincidental to my mind." Look up the word in any dictionary, and you will see that the origin of Witch and Witchcraft stem from the Anglo-Saxon words *wicce,* feminine, and *wicca,* masculine. The word *witan* is the plural of the Anglo Saxon *wita,* which means a sage or wise one, a counselor; *witan,* meaning "wise men," were members of the king's council who helped him in administrative and judicial matters. Dictionaries give the correct etymology of the word, but their definitions of course are biased, since they were compiled by Judeo-Christians. Graham's definition of witchcraft is not only etymologically incorrect but his motives unethical.

What Billy Graham is saying is that all those people, all those religions, who don't accept the Christian Bible as "Gospel truth" (a contradiction in terms) are agents of the Devil. In this light, it's not hard to understand why as a spiritual leader with free access to the media he never once spoke out against the atrocities committed on North Vietnam by our American bombers, which dropped more tons of bombs on that small country than in all of World Wars I and II. Most of the Catholic North Vietnamese fled to the South because during the French occupation they sided with them and were considered traitors. Thus those who were left were either atheists, Communists, or members of those "Eastern religions" that he has denounced. As for those Bibleless peasants—bombs away!

Graham claims that the increase in drugs, mass murder, pornography, sexual license, and everything else that is evil in this country is connected to the occult, especially "witchcraft." I suggest that he and his coreligionists reread their own Bible. There is more filth, pillage, rape, murder, sacrifice of innocent human beings, and bloody examples of man's inhumanity to man in that book than in any of the most depraved of modern novels. It would take a book twice this size for me to point them out chapter and verse. Then too, if the Bible is "the living word of God," that God is totally unreliable, one who is constantly contradicting Himself. The Bible's wording is so vague that we now have hundreds of different and opposing churches calling themselves Christian, all claiming to base their beliefs on the "Good Book." When Graham says, "All of us engaged in Christian work are constantly aware of the fact that we have to do battle with supernatural forces and powers. The Devil follows me every day. He tempts me. He is a very real presence to me," I believe him. And one of the temptations he and his fellow religionists have never been able to resist is the "bearing of false witness against thy neighbor" in his attacks on the Old Religion, which in itself is a betrayal of the very Bible he upholds.

As the saying goes, "As ye sow so shall ye reap." Graham and those who think like him have planted the seeds of the Devil in their own minds, nurtured them throughout their lives, and now are reaping a full harvest. What they can't understand—or refuse to—is that practitioners of true Witchcraft, the Old Religion, not only have never planted any Satanic seeds, they don't even believe in their existence. And the wars, mass murders, rapes, and increase in drug-related crimes, can't possibly stem from Witchcraft, since we haven't been the dominant power for nearly two thousand years. It's the failure of Judeo-Christianity, operating on a false premise, offering man a heavenly reward while he goes through hell on earth, a philosophy based on sanctified sadomasochism which constantly demands the sacrifice of self or others, its symbol the cross on which their Christ was crucified, where everything that is good and natural and joyous and life-sustaining has been perverted into a "sin," where a Christian commences this life with the idea that his very existence is the result of a shameful or sinful sexual act and the propagation of the race requires further "sinful" acts, where one's biologically natural needs are biblically opposed, where pie in the sky is offered to those who are starving on earth (the Christian version of Marie Antoinette's "let them eat cake"), where those who most vocally defend their faith are usually the ones who least practice it, where our prisons are full of people who were brought up as Christians but lost their faith and their way because they saw the hypocrisies, the money-changers in the temple that Jesus whipped, the spiritual leaders more concerned with temporal rather than temple matters, and that no matter what Bible quotes were used, it was obvious that the chief deity of them all was the almighty dollar.

The attack on the occult, and Witchcraft in particular, is an evasion of their own responsibility for the spiritual sewer that exists today. And if they want to blame the Devil, using comedian Flip Wilson's funny "The Devil made me do it," they should acknowledge that it's the Devil of their own creation, the symbol of the evil that rests in their own souls because of a schizophrenic theology. If "there's the Devil to pay," let those who have created and believe in him do the paying.

Unlike the Biblical God, the deities of the Witches don't sanction slavery. In my book *How To Prevent Psychic Blackmail* I give many examples in the chapter entitled "Blackmail By The Bible." Here's one of them from Leviticus 25:44–46: "As for your male and female slaves whom you may have; you may buy male and female slaves from among the nations that are round you. You may also buy from among the strangers who sojourn with you and their families that are with you, who have been born in your land; and they may be your property. You may bequeath them to your sons and after you, to inherit as a possession forever; you may make slaves of them, but over your brethren the people of Israel you shall not rule, one over the other, with harshness."

Witch Martello totally agrees with atheist Madalyn Murray O'Hair in wanting the Bible to be studied in public schools. Bible study in this instance is not a synonym for prayer in public schools. And if Christians like Billy Graham tried to implement all that their Bible advocates, the U.S. government would be forced to jail them all. It's not a theocracy—yet. For instance, the Bible advocates death for all of the following: consulting wizards (Leviticus 20:6), idolatry or heresy (Exodus 22:20), Sabbath-breaking (Exodus 32:14–15), kindling a fire on the seventh day (Exodus 35:2–3), not keeping the Passover Feast (Numbers 9:13), eating unleavened bread during Passover (Exodus 12:15), eating fat (Leviticus 7:22–25), making perfume (Exodus 30:34–38), killing cattle without bringing an offering to the priests (Leviticus 17:2–5), and touching a holy thing (Numbers 4:15). And on and on ad nauseam. And what about King Solomon, who is thus described in I Kings 11:1–3: "But King Solomon loved many strange women . . . . and he had seven hundred wives, princesses, and three hundred concubines: and his wives turned away his heart"?

The best ammunition against these theological bullies is their own Bible. If it's the true word of God, why isn't Billy Graham living up to it? Why doesn't he go out and murder all those people who don't keep the Sabbath, who make perfume, or who kindle a fire on the seventh day? Why doesn't he openly preach the divine right to slavery, especially to the blacks in this country? Was his silence during the Vietnam War his way of implementing the above biblical quotes, his Graham-cracker method of letting Uncle Sam do it? Either he practices what he preaches or he is a hypocrite.

This book is not written for those who are interested primarily in hexes, spells, curses, and the Judeo-Christian idea of what Witchcraft is. It is not a how-to book. The good ones will be mentioned in the text. It is an attempt to show some of the roots of the Old Religion as practiced today by Witches of many different traditions. I have eliminated much of the Inquisitional "cases" and history, because they've been done to death and the reading and the writing of them makes me physically ill. I've tried to show the differences between true Witches, Old Religionists, Pop Witches, Christian-defined Witches, and Satanists. I have shown how our Horned God existed prior to the advent of Judeo-Christianity and how our Mother Goddess was incorporated into the Catholic Church under a different name (although her name itself is one of the many variations of the Goddess's name, such as Mari or Marian). I have also tried to show that contrary to Christian claims that Witches have perverted their rites, it's the Christians who have plagiarized and perverted our ancient rites and feast days.

I am a Witch by family tradition, by initiation, by choice, and by my love of our Horned God and Mother Goddess. I work and worship not only with my own tradition—Sicilian—but with four others as well: Continental, traditional, Welsh traditionalist, and Pagan. I love and respect each of them. I'm also very close to some other traditions, including the Gardnerian and the Alexandrian, whose priests and priestesses are personal friends. I've participated in many coven circles, both indoors and outdoors. After all the traditions have been put aside, all the labels stripped, I found that we are all Witches under the skin. There are also a few so-called Witches that I thoroughly despise. Fortunately, they are in the minority.

On February 2, 1973, Olmelc or Candlemas, the Welsh traditionalist covens of New York presented me with a magnificent Wolf's Head Silver Chalice "in appreciation for all that you have done for us and as our third-degree Elder." The Wolf's Head is a symbol of the third degree in their tradition.

The occult boom in recent years, especially interest in Witchcraft of whatever variety and designation, has caused alarm in the major religions. Even from a financial standpoint they feel it's a threat: The occult coffers are full while their collection plates are empty—as are their churches. They launch vast proselytizing campaigns to gain new recruits. Their spiritual henchmen write vicious attacks on the Old Religion. Yet we don't actively seek converts. We don't need big churches. Any glen or glade will do. Or an apartment.

And when we leave our coven, we're all spiritually high, happy, healthy. We are there voluntarily, not by guilt or obligation. Our prayers and our rituals are done not by rote but in total reverence. We have no fear of an avenging God (and in our case Goddess), no horror of hell, and unlike so many others, absolutely no sense of evil. In fact, our covens enable us to escape the evils of the world, to experience a sense of oneness and compassion and sharing and joy denied to those who have accepted a hellbent theology. When it comes to my religion—The Old Religion—I suffer from chronic happiness. It's not surprising to find that those who lack this in their own faith should be jealous and hostile. I leave them to their own "one God" and their multitudes of devils.

In the Craft there is no hard dogma. Hard drugs are forbidden. Mindless morons can't be a compliment to our Mother Goddess. Sex is sacred, not something to be exhibited at a peep show. Power is something personal, not to be used over others, which is contrary to Craft ethics. Those who think the Old Religion will make them masters over others are slaves to their own self-delusions. A happy person is always a powerful person and is hated by those who aren't. A happy person is in many ways selfish: In the Craft we must protect our best interests and insure that the power that comes from joy remains constant, knowing that none of us are immune from the vicissitudes of life, but that our Old Religion will help us to handle any adversity. The Craft has survived for thousands of years. After everything else has come and gone, it will remain. And one day, in the coming Age of Aquarius, there will once again be magnificent temples to the Goddess.

1

Witchcraft: Old Religion, New Revolution

Witchcraft, the Old Religion, may be the faith of the future. All over the world Witches are coming out of their broomclosets to sweep away the church-induced prejudices and fears against it. Modern witchcraft is undergoing many radical changes. Sacred cows are being challenged. Old terms are being updated. And for the first time in history, modern Witches are fighting for their constitutionally guaranteed civil rights.

The world's first public Witch-In was held on Halloween, October 31, 1970, in New York's Central Park. The event was made into a documentary film by Global Village and shown many times on Channel 13, New York's National Educational Television outlet. When the Witches International Craft Associates (WICA) filed for a permit to hold their Witch-In, they were refused by the city Parks Department. They refused to accept the arbitrary reasons given for the refusal and were prepared for any eventuality. Let me quote from their publication, *The WICA Newsletter:*

> Dr. Martello and WICA applied to the New York City Parks Dept. for a Witch-In Permit. Call came: "Permission denied." I asked the reason. Man hostile, saying, "It does not serve the purpose of the park." I said, "I thought the park existed to serve the purpose of the people. Anyway, we will congregate for our Witch-In as *Individuals*. Even witches have civil rights." At that he said, "I'll inform the police." At that threat of police harrassment and possible arrest I called the American Civil Liberties Union, New York. Mrs. Barbara Shack of the NYCLU took our case on personally, backed completely by ACLU. On Thursday, October 29, 1970, two days before our Witch-In, she and I met with the City Parks Attorney and its Deputy Commissioner. They were most cordial and reversed their original refusal and gave us a Permit in Writing. They wanted to change the wording of Witch-In. I refused, saying, "Since the Sheep Meadow in Central Park once had sheep, and since the symbolic God of the witches is a goat, what could be more appropriate? It's a good thing I didn't apply for a Permit for a Goat-In!"

WICA threatened to file a civil rights suit against the New York City Parks Department for discrimination against a minority religion, backed by the American Civil Liberties Union, if it didn't get the Witch-In permit. This constitutes the first civil-rights victory for witches. The Witch-In drew over a thousand people with dozens of reporters, photographers, and TV cameras. Witches and non-Witches held hands, forming an ever-widening circle, and danced the Witches Reel, singing an old Wiccan tune, "London Bridge Is Falling Down," with new words composed by a Connecticut witch: "Witches meet in Central Park, Central Park, Central Park, Witches meet in Central Park for Our Lady."

"Our Lady," of course, is the Goddess. The Old Religion has always worshipped both a Horned God, known as Cernunnos, Pan, and other names, symbol of the hunt, during winter, and the Goddess, generally known as Diana, but with many other names, symbol of fertility and harvest, during the summer months. Halloween is the time when the rulership of the Craft passes from the Goddess to the God.

Female witches have always been held in high honor, often heading their own covens. The Old Religion is probably the only one that hasn't discriminated against women by keeping them in inferior ecclesiastical positions. In many branches of the Craft the Goddess is superior to the male God; in others they're equal, and a few branches emphasize the male Horned God. The female witch has always been a liberated woman, living her life in her own way and not just as an appendage to the man. This is one of the reasons why many in the Women's Liberation Movement support the Old Religion. Quite a few are Craft members themselves, and they have backed the Witches Liberation Movement to the hilt.

The Witches Liberation Movement has been formed for the following reasons: For centuries Witchcraft has been the garbage heap upon which all the moral refuse of other people has been dumped. The Old Religion has been vilified, perjured about, twisted, persecuted, and prosecuted, not because of what it was (and is), but because of what the Church said it was. Nearly all of the books written about it were authored by non-Witches. The early *grimoires* (Witch grammars) were written by Christian ecclesiasts with their own religious axes to grind. False, fanatic, and without fact, these books, and those that followed, infallibly linked Witchcraft to devil worship. In support of this they produced the "confessions" of tortured "Witches" who claimed intercourse with Satan, Sabbath orgies, and other drug-induced nonsense. Most of these poor souls were deluded non-Witches who were tortured into confessing almost anything to relieve their agony. Also lending credence to the belief in the adoration of the Devil, was the fact that the God of the Witches was horned, a god and symbol going back to paleolithic times, thousands of years before Christ was born. Thus the Craft God became the Christian Devil.

Christian brainwashing has been so effective that even today the general view of Witchcraft is the one fostered by the Catholic Church. This is true even of atheists, who don't believe in God, let alone any church. Yet they would be surprised to learn that their reaction to what Witchcraft is all about is precisely the one created and desired by the early Church. Religious intolerance takes many forms; the laws against Witchcraft constitute discrimination against a minority religion. Furthermore, they are unconstitutional in a secular society that guarantees freedom of religion (and from religion). And of course these laws were made by Christians. The same people, especially writers, who wouldn't dare call the blackman in America "nigger" are the same ones who are doing just that every time they link the Old Religion with devil worship. These journalistic bigots continue to repeat "The Big Lie" and are involuntary Inquisitional henchmen. Either they don't know the facts, or what is morally worse, they choose to ignore them. Witches don't believe in the Devil or Heaven or Hell. The only people who can be true Satanists are Christians: They believe in the Devil, in Hell, in the concept of evil. Thus devil-worshippers are nothing but reverse or perverse Christians. They represent the dark side of Christianity (as did the movie *Rosemary's Baby*). This is another instance where Christians have used Witches as the scapegoat for their own suppressed fears and failings. They did the same thing to the black man in their desperate attempts to exhibit a lily-white soul. The Christian child is taught that every time he commits a "sin" a "black mark" is left on his soul. It's not hard to see how as an adult anything associated with "black" becomes automatically "bad" and anything with "white" is "good." A few examples: Black Magic . . . Black Mass . . . Blackmail . . . Black widow (spider) . . . Black mark . . . Blackguard . . . Blackman?

This is one of the reasons why the Witches Liberation Movement has been formed. References to someone being a "white Witch" or a "black Witch" indicate unconscious racism. Tradition is not a substitute for truth. Black is no longer a synonym for bad any more than white is a synonym for good. We prefer the terms "bad" or "good" or "positive" or "negative."

Also being challenged are such terms as "righthand path" and "lefthand path," denoting good Witchcraft and bad Witchcraft. We all know the suffering lefthanded children have had to undergo—needlessly. The continued use of these terms indicates unfair discrimination, whether unintentional, or not, against people who are lefthanded.

Old prejudices die hard. This is why we have consciousness-raising groups and insist that all WICA members do a great deal of soul-searching, to make sure that they do not continue to propagate an unconscious prejudice through the use of outdated stereotyped terms.

Many of the highly publicized Witches are considered "Uncle Toms" by those in the Craft. They are capitalizing on the secret fears, hopes, and prejudices of the public—living down to the "images" expected of them, rather than living up to the true Craft standards. We object not to the publicity per se but to some of the false statements which only stigmatize true Witches. They are basically leeches and religious prostitutes, taking advantage of the current interest in the Old Religion, getting all they can out of belief in the Craft and putting nothing into it. Because of Karmic law we know their days are numbered, but we don't intend to be penalized because of their misdeeds.

Witchcraft has been and still is a moral no man's land. Its very autonomy and secrecy are both blessings and burdens. They are blessings in that the covens are limited to the traditional thirteen, so that all members can take an active part; their secrecy enables them to worship without fear, to "do their thing," to keep the power intact by not exposing it to public gaze. They are burdens in that all covens are independent and most of them unknown to each other (wise during Inquisitional times), which prevents them from being able to demand their religious and civil rights or from using the courts effectively. Without a strong organization,

Witchcraft: Old Religion, New Revolution

the Old Religion exists as thousands of isolated cells, alienated from each other and the public. The old traditional diehards oppose publicity, and this is not without merit. Yet this is also the very thing that enables unscrupulous opportunists to grab the headlines and make irresponsible statements to the press. These opportunists jump at the opportunity further to denigrate the Craft by publicizing self-dubbed Witches, but they shy away from the real issues involved: civil rights, religious freedom, historical accuracy.

The new trend in Witchcraft is for organization and cooperation between the various groups, though each one retains its own autonomy. Unfortunately, there are some prima donnas who have a vested interest in keeping the Craft divided. They really don't care about the Old Religion—just what they can get out of it. They have taken no stands, fought no battles, offered no solutions. They publicize Witchcraft as the Old Religion but do nothing to implement their claims. If they truly believe in the Old Religion, why do they still keep it in the realm of disrespect? Today the Craft is fair game for anyone: They can distort its truth, vilify its practitioners, write religious racist articles, produce sensationalized TV shows, all with impunity. And who makes this possible? The Witches themselves! Until they raise their consciousness, come out of their broom closets, challenge every statement written about the Craft, defend their religious beliefs, they are giving the sanction of the victim—furnishing their oppressors with the weapons for their own destruction.

Rather than indulging in the competitive ego-trips of some groups, WICA is made up of members of many diverse groups who take action, if only by writing letters, every time the true Craft is attacked. Currently being set up with legal assistance is the Witches Anti-Defamation League. As far as we're concerned, to talk about Witchcraft power and having no guts is a contradiction in terms.

Among the eight points listed in *The Witch Manifesto* in my book *Weird Ways of Witchcraft* is the following: "Witches Protest Demonstrations, Marches, Rallies to be given a legal permit by the city in which they occur. Failure or refusal to do so by any city indicates religious discrimination and will be fought in the courts. Just as most cities permit St. Patrick's Day parades, a saint whose authenticity is now in dispute, a religious march secularly sanctioned, Witches have the same right to a Witches Day and a Witches Parade."

The above point was implemented when WICA filed for a Witch-In permit for their main religious holiday, Halloween, October 31, 1970—a holiday stolen and celebrated by the public, yet denied to those to whom it belongs. As liberated Witches, we had no intention of taking this lying down. We fought. We won. That's the first shot in a long battle for full religious freedom. The public relations job is tremendous: to challenge every single statement by "authorities" linking the Old Religion with Christian deviltry or psychedelic drugs; to weed out those sick individuals who think that our religion is a refuge for the psychotic, the incompetent, or the morally bankrupt; and most important of all, to help genuine Witches to free themselves of any kind of self-doubt instilled by an oppressive society.

When the last public census was taken, Witches belonging to Continental covens listed under religion: Wiccan. This requires semantic clarification. The words *wit* and *witch* are derived from old Anglo-Saxon *wicca*, meaning "wise"; thus, wicca-craft, wit-craft, witchcraft. There are two kinds of Witches (though a number of different sects): hereditary and initiated. There are people who believe in and follow the Old Religion but who are not themselves Witches, strictly speaking. Most followers of Christianity are themselves neither priests nor ministers. They're called Christians. Non-Witch followers of the Old Religion are called Wiccans. In the covens all members take an active part, each member a priest or priestess, presided over by a Magister or High Priest and High Priestess, often three in number. The secret rites and secret names of our God and Goddess are known only to the initiated. This secrecy has been cause for suspicion, but it exists in order to preserve the Old Mysteries, to keep the cone of power intact, to keep the Craft clean—just as Catholics are unaware of what takes place in the *inner sanctum* of the College of Cardinals.

The renaissance of the Old Religion (as opposed to Witchcraft as a cult for the curious) is both evolutionary and revolutionary in these troubled times. Its emergence after centuries of existence as an underground spring coincides with movements all over the world fighting for self-determination. It fills the spiritual gap left by organized religion. It coexists with the revival of paganism in the most positive sense of that word: of the country, in tune with nature, compatible with modern ecologists whose emphasis on conservation has always been one of the tenets of Old Religionists. Witches have always worked with the super possibilities in the natural: nature cures, herbs, mind power (suggestion, hypnosis, telepathy, psychic ability). Far from being supernaturalists, they have been able to use highly concentrated thought and energy in order to achieve results. The ritualized use of athames (sacred knives), cord, cups, sword, pentagrams, pentacles, candles, incense, caldrons, wands, salt, and other paraphernalia all help to induce a state of intense concentration, mentally directed and emotionally experienced, enabling Witches to work their wonders.

Some of these same principles exist in other therapies and religions, such as faith cures, prayer, hypnotherapy, and positive thinking. Christian Scientists would have apoplexy if told that they are using Witchcraft techniques enveloped in the banner of "acceptable" nomenclature: "Christian" Science. We prefer our own Wicca Art—the Old Religion—and have no intention of making it more "palatable" to public prejudice.

The very fact that many religions would vehemently deny any association with the Craft in any form shows just how deep the prejudice is. If you dig deep enough, however, you will find that the substrata of many religions are based on the Craft of the Wise. Many of the old Christian churches were built upon sites used for the Old Religion. Pope Gregory issued an edict to the effect that where such places of "pagan" worship were too strong to uproot, Catholic churches should be built. Throughout Europe, notably in England, you can still see traces of the Old Religion built right into the churches: Images of the Horned God and the Great Earth Mother, pentagrams, and other Witch marks, put there by ostensible "Christians" who were really followers of the Old Faith.

The Old Religion has been and still is one of the most persecuted minorities in the world. For this reason our fight is on many fronts: religion, civil rights, public relations, education, organization, psychology. Because of public misunderstanding and the nature of

Witchcraft: Old Religion, New Revolution

our religion, some of us are forced to go to the public via lectures and articles to help clarify things. I myself made sure that I was professionally secure as a writer, lecturer, and graphologist before "going public." Even some of my closest friends didn't know that I belonged to a coven of Continental Witches, even though they often jokingly called me a "witch." (*Witch* is the correct term for both sexes, though *warlock* seems to be preferred by the American non-Witch public.) My ancestry is Sicilian, and I'm in constant touch with covens there. The *strege* (Witches) in our family go back for centuries. My grandmother used to read the old *Tarocchi* deck of cards, from which we get the modern Tarot. She was the village *strega* and both envied and hated by the priests. My distant relative Count Cagliostro, né Giuseppe Balsamo (his paternal grandparents were Matteo and Maria Martello), was strangled by church friars in the dungeons of San Leo, Italy. His wife Serafina was buried in a nunnery. (News of this was published in the *Miniteur Universal,* October 6, 1795.) Two books on Cagliostro that give his family history mentioning my namesakes are *Cagliostro: Scoundrel Or Saint?* by François Ribadeau Dumas, and *Cagliostro* by W. R. H. Trowbridge.

Witchcraft, the Old Religion, is now in the forefront of a spiritual revolution that will reach its apex during the Aquarian Age. We in WICA, the Witches Liberation Movement, and the Witches Anti-Defamation League, don't consider ourselves "leaders" but rather apostles for the Old Religion. We have no illusions about people's deeply ingrained prejudices. It's not even necessary to try to change them. But we will see to it that our civil rights are legally protected by using the laws of the land just like everyone else.

2

Pioneers of Witchcraft's New Renaissance

Witchcraft has emerged from an underground religion practiced in secrecy to an overground "pop culture." When the last of the Witchcraft laws was repealed in England in 1951, Witches started to come out of their broomclosets. When Gerald B. Gardner's *Witchcraft Today* was published in 1954, he got letters from all over Britain and other countries from people who said that they were Witches and belonged to covens. Many believed that they were the only ones in existence. Whether fact or fantasy, these letters did reveal a deep emotional and spiritual need—not only a feeling but a desperate craving for the old ways—a Jungian collective unconscious and racial memory triggered off by Gardner's book.

CHARLES GODFREY LELAND

Prior to Gardner's emergence, there were two other authors who contributed to the Witchcraft revival. The first of these was Charles Godfrey Leland, founder and first president of the Gypsy Lore Society, prolific author and folklorist extraordinaire. His theories and writing on the unconscious, the subliminal self, and dreams predated those of Sigmund Freud. He wrote dozens of books and thousands of articles. Born in Philadelphia, he later went to England and spent his remaining years in Florence, Italy, where he died on March 20, 1903, at the age of seventy-eight.

Leland was highly pleased that he was born on August 15, 1824, for that's the date attributed to the ascension into heaven of both Buddha and the Blessed Virgin Mary. He considered himself very fortunate. Attracted to the odd and the unusual at an early age, he later wrote in his *Memoirs*: "As it occurs to me, the spirit which was over Philadelphia in my boyhood, houses, gardens, people, and their life, was strangely quiet, sunny, and quaint, a dream of olden time drawn into modern days. The Quaker predominated, and his memories were mostly in the past; ours, as I have often said, was a city of great trees, which seemed to me to be ever repeating their old poetic legends to the wind, of Swedes, witches, and Indians."

In her two-volume biography of Leland, his niece, Elizabeth Robins Pennell, writes: "Nor was the marvelous ever very far away. Not only did statues walk, but there were great marble dogs in Race Street by which the small boy who was wise ran quickly, for they howled when anybody in the neighbourhood died; a dreadful sound, surely, even for grown-up people to hear. Then, there were Indians who came from their graves to hold their weekly market in Independence Square, and, had he only waked at the midnight hour, he might (who knows?) have seen, from the Fifth Street windows, the statue of Franklin stalking among their shadows. There was the Quaker girl, too, whose ghost on summer nights wandered among the flowers in the garden of the old Pennington House, a ghost no one need have been afraid of. These and other pleasant terrors lurked at every corner, in every open place of the town. In the quiet parlour at home he heard of worse than ghosts. For often the gossip of his mother and her friends, over their tea, went back to the days before Penn, when there was no Quaker City on the banks of the Delaware, but a little colony of Swedes, and the women were mostly witches who would go flying off on broomsticks to join in the revels on the Hudson. No one knew this gossip better, or had more awful tales to tell, than Miss Eliza Leslie, who wrote the most practical cookbook ever published, and one of the most popular, too, as I have learned to my cost, the first edition being beyond reach. If an authoress of such strong common sense could believe in these things, what was to be expected of the small boy who tremblingly hung on her every word? And when he invested in Dime Novels of the day, half the time it was to read some horror of the Salem witches; when he wandered into the kitchen, Irish servants whispered of fairies, or old coloured women muttered 'voodoo incantations.' Once there was, a cook, who had gone so far as to put 'a spell of death' on all who dared to take her place."

Leland's father, Henry, was of Puritan stock, a descendant of Hopestill Leland, who was the first white settler in New England. His forebears included the De Bussli who came from Normandy with the Conqueror to England and in gratitude was given the Leland manor from which their descendants took their name. Another ancestor was Charles Leland, secretary of the Society of Antiquaries during the reign of Charles I. His mother's family was an intermixture of Puritan and Huguenot stock, and Leland liked to recall that one ancestress married a "High German," a doctor with a reputation for sorcery: "My mother's opinion was that this was a very strong case of atavism, and that the mysterious ancestor had through the ages cropped out in me." He believed that he was Washington Irving's "High German doctor" who laid the mystic spell on Sleepy Hollow. His maternal grandfather, Colonel Godfrey, moved to Massachusetts after fighting in the Revolutionary War and became an aide-de-camp to the governor.

As a young boy Leland had an affinity with nature, a rapport with Gypsies, an empathy for oppressed people. He was a voracious reader, but at eighteen, as he said: "Occult literature had the upper hand." He had an old manuscript copy of *Pemander of Trismegistus* with "Transcribed by Charles Leland, 1842." He was eighteen. He delved into Transcendentalism, and his mother had even visited Brook Farm. Even as a child he had written, "I am I. I am Myself. I myself I." His school days weren't generally happy ones. However, he attended one school run by Bronson and Hunt Alcott. The latter would be considered progressive today; he introduced the young Leland to Cornelius Agrippa's works, long classics in the occult. He believed in teaching by "moral influence" and a "sympathetic intellectual communion." Leland said, "He encouraged me to read everything and to learn almost nothing. . . . Such a training as his would develop in any boy certain weaknesses—and I had mine—which were very repulsive to my father, who carried plain common sense to extremes and sometimes into its opposite of unconscious eccentricity, though there was no word which he so much hated."

At seventeen Charles Godfrey Leland entered Princeton University and graduated four years later, once being "expelled" with his whole class for "rebellion." He hated it and agreed with a writer in the *Nassau Monthly* that if he achieved success as an author, it was in spite of his college days. When he returned to Philadelphia, his father suggested a stay in Europe "for both health and study reasons." Once in Europe, he got into what proper Philadelphians would indeed call bad company. Yet he was fascinated with Spanish smugglers, meeting an old slave-trader and pirate, mingling with the Apaches and denizens of the demimonde. He listened attentively to the songs of troubadours, from Provence and Marseilles to Naples, and then to Genoa, Rome, Florence, and Venice. He wrote glowing letters of his adventures to his family, especially to his brother Henry. They are full of a child's sense of wonder, full of details and minute descriptions of the people and the places visited. His was a constant search for the marvelous. He had a genius for penetrating the ordinary and discovering the unusual. He enrolled at the university at Heidelberg, Germany, and discovered "once and for all, that I have no gift for mathematics." He did have gifts for German beer and "debauchery." At this time he "grew vigorous and healthy, or, as the saying is, 'hearty as a buck.'"

In Germany he was exposed to hexerei. He visited

Munich, Berlin, Nuremberg, Dresden, Vienna, Holland, Belgium, Poland, Russia, and Paris, especially the latter's Latin Quarter. And he was in the midst of the French Revolution. In one of his long letters to his father describing the Revolution, he included a small printed circular addressed to: "Monsieur C. G. Leland, 62 Rue de la Harpe" which today in itself is a historical document. It read:

> Sir,—A meeting of citizens of the United States of America will take place at No. 9 Rue Richer tomorrow, March 2nd, at 12 o'clock, to make arrangements for a proper expression of feeling to the Provisional Government of France in respect of the recent revolution.
> You are respectfully invited to attend, and particularly requested to notify your American friends of said meeting.
> Paris, 1st March, 1848.

Leland returned to America, continued his education, and upon graduation opened an office as an attorney. That lasted six months. He began writing for many publications, including one published by the circus entrepreneur P. T. Barnum in New York. He once wrote, "Uncle Barnum was always good as gold to me." After that he became editor of the Philadelphia *Bulletin*. He wrote fiery antislavery articles. He was an abolitionist. He had no patience with compromise. His writings provoked the wrath of many, especially Southern editors. When he got married, he made sure that there were two ministers present: the presiding Bishop Wilbur and, unbeknownst to the others, a black minister serving as one of the waiters. His reputation enabled him to meet the great literary figures of the day—Emerson, Holmes, Longfellow, Lowell, Agassiz—and his *Ballad of Hans Breitmann,* done in a humorous verse with all of the German pronunciations of English words, such as "Hans Breitmann gife a barty; Vhere ish dot barty now?" gained him international fame. But later many identified him with the beer-drinking character of the *Ballad,* who was totally dissimilar, and it often proved most annoying to him.

After his mother, brother, and father had died, leaving him comfortably off, he decided to go to England, where a publisher planned to publish his *Ballad of Hans Breitmann.* Heretofore his works had been pirated in England and on the Continent. The year was 1869. For the next ten years his home base was in England, his friends Gypsies and autocrats, where he lived a Jekyll-Hyde existence. He was forty-five. He took many trips to Russia, all over the Continent, and even to Egypt. To his family and friends, ever since boyhood, he was called the Rye. He wrote of his adventures in "Russian Gypsies" and "The Egyptian Sketch Book." His many articles were incorporated into the book *The Gypsies,* published in 1882 in America.

In a letter dated December 17, 1871, to Mrs. John Harrison, Leland said, "I am following up my Gypsies with great success and have one regular Romany Chal who passes Saturdays with me. I am really getting to talk the language quite well and could write you a letter in it. Nobody ever yet, except Borrow, got into their good graces so, and they tell me their tricks and secrets without reserve."

Of interest to Witches of Celtic tradition is this passage from a letter to Mrs. Harrison dated September 7, 1872: "And thin we wint to Killarney, and sure we

Pioneers of Witchcraft's New Renaissance 41

had a great time, and saw the place where St. Patrick drowndhed the snakes in a bit of a lake, an' it was mysilf—praise the Lord!—that diskivired an owld Irish Ogham inscription in the ruins of Agadoe, which I copied and sint to my friend Dochthor Caulfield, the principle of the Royal Cork Insthitution—it's he that's a gintleman!—And thin we wint to Correckan, thin to Blarney, where I kissed the Blarney Stone (Belle didn't go up) and thin thro' siviral places to Galway, and the Giant's Causeway. An' there I got two owld Irish axe heads of stone and two arry hids an a bade from an owld tomb. And we had a beautiful day and saw the sanery and an owld ruin, an' firin wid a rifle I hit the bull's eye at 55 yards—the saints be good to me."

During Leland's stay in England he traveled everywhere and knew everyone from the poet Robert Browning to George Eliot to Bulwer Lytton to members of royalty. He was on intimate terms with English, Irish, and Scotch Gypsies. The tinkers were his friends. He was lionized. Yet in 1879 he returned to Philadelphia, where he was once again caught up in the social and literary life of the country. In his niece's biography of him she says, "What impressed me most in his talk was its great range and his great seriousness. He had no small talk. He talked of everything except everyday topics. He was discussing the Philosophy of the Will, or the Religion of Agnosticism, at the point where conversation usually dallies with the weather. Darwin, Huxley, Carpenter were names oftener in his mouth than those of the heroes and heroines of the newest scandal. His was gossip that led to metaphysical depths before you knew where you were, and the amulet drawn from his pocket was of more importance that the latest despatch in the latest edition of the afternoon paper.

And there was no resisting his seriousness. All his thought, all his energy was concentrated upon what he was saying: it was a matter of life and death to him; and his manner was as fascinating as the deep blue eyes that held you as he carried on his argument or elaborated his description. His voice was low and slightly sonorous."

"Life is a romance," Leland once said, "to everybody who observes it." Nothing escaped him. He could best be described as a practical mystic. He established the Industrial Art School in Philadelphia. Later he wrote a book on his teaching methods. He wrote, lectured, and edited magazines and books. He wrote a pamphlet for the U.S. Bureau of Education that was used throughout the country. His ideas were implemented all over the United States, but few gave him credit for them. The summers of 1881, 1882, and 1883, Leland spent with American Indians in their own tents; as Miss Pennell wrote, "The hours in their tents by the sea helped to give him courage for the routine of work in Philadelphia. The quiet, industrious, civilised Passamaquoddies danced no war dances with him,— led him on no wild chase across the plains. As I saw them, they were tranquility itself. But the old fire, the old wildness, the old magic was in their legends, and in each, as he forced it from them by his own spell of sympathy, he drew a fresh breath of life. I remember what splendid form he was always in when he got back to Philadelphia and to work in the fall, his note-book full of Indian words and phrases and stories, his trunk full of birch-bark boxes. The procession of savages, armed with tomahawks, grasping each other's long hair, that encircled some of the boxes, proved to me how well the Indians had been initiated into the mystery of spirals."

What distinguished Leland from all other scholars was his genuine love of the Indian, The Gypsy, and the Witch. He was called the Romany Rye. Having learned the Gypsy language in England, he delighted in astonishing Gypsies in America, and later in Hungary, Italy, Russia, and Egypt, by speaking it—especially since his over six-foot, white-skinned, blue-eyed stature made him the complete *gorgio,* or Gentile. In Paris he told the Hungarian Gypsies their forture in their own language. His was an imposing, patriarchal presence. And unlike most ivory-tower sociologists today who rarely met, and never lived, with the people they describe, Leland was always one of the people.

Leland stayed in Philadelphia four years, then returned to England. He began the *Gypsy Lore Journal,* the forerunner of the Gypsy Lore Society of which he was founder and first president. He wrote and compiled the *Book of English Gypsy Songs,* a collection of Romany Ballads. In 1889 he attended the Folk-Lore Congress in Paris and later the Oriental Congress in Stockholm. He even wrote the coronation speech for the King of the Gypsies, crowned at Tetholm, in 1898. He learned to speak Romany, Shelta, and Welsh. David MacRitchie's pamphlet on "The Cairds' Language," published in the late 1800s, says, "Its discoverer, and the one who first proclaimed his discovery to the public, was an American man of letters, Mr. Charles Godfrey Leland, who throughout his life took a keen interest in all kinds of out-of-the-way forms of speech." The Chambers' Encyclopedia describes his discovery of Shelta: "The earliest specimens of this idiom were collected (1877–80) by Mr. C. G. Leland from an English vagrant in North Wales and an Irish tinker in Philadelphia." Mr. MacRitchie had also contributed an article on this subject called "Shelta: The Cairds'

Language," published in the *Transactions of the Gaelic Society of Inverness* (Volume 24, 1899–1901). What is fascinating in all this is that Shelta was identified with Ogham.

In 1888 he wrote the following letter to his niece from Florence:

> An English lady told me a day or two ago that she believed I was the Wandering Jew—ever going on—always in new adventure. Yes, 'tis even so: *ohne Rast, ohne Ruh*. And I have such a budget to unfold. I pass over the Gypsies in Vienna and the meeting of old friends, etc. But at Budapest I had a grand campaign. On the second day, I was taken to the Roman ruined city of Acquaquintum by the Danube to see a really wonderful mosaic representing wrestlers. "That thing to the left," said the *custos*, "represents an *ampulla*. But what that is to the right, neither Pulsky, nor Hampel, nor the devil himself can tell." Then I spoke and said, "I am not the devil—but I say they were *stigiles*—or implements used in baths to scrape the skin." There were three archaeologists present, and the next day it was in the newspapers that a great American archaeologist, "a man of imposing stature with a long grey waving beard," had solved the great mystery.
>
> Then the greatest Folk Lore Society in the world, with 14 sub-divisions, was founded (Hungarian, Armenian, Yiddish, Gypsy, Wallach, Croat, Serb, Spanish, etc.), and I was the first member nominated.
>
> Then the Ethnological Society gave me a reception, wherein Prof. Herrmann delivered an

Pioneers of Witchcraft's New Renaissance 45

address all about me and my works and glorified me as the President of the British Gypsy-Lore Society—I did not (fortunately) understand a word of it, as it was in Hungarian, but it must have been very touching, to judge from the admiration of your uncle which was expressed.

Finally, I found my system of the Minor Arts in 50 public schools in Hungary, and it is usually recognised there now as mine. And I succeeded in inducing a few very intelligent and able men who had already read my *Practical Education* to study it and form a body with a view of testing the whole system. . . .

I wonder where all our wandering will end. I could almost live in Florence. I felt that my last 6 months in Italy were wasted—but now I have a prospect to do good in the schools. . . .

His niece wrote, "He did live, not almost, but altogether in Florence, as it turned out, and he accomplished there much good, though not exactly of the kind expected. It was this winter he was initiated into the Witch-Lore of the Romagna, an initiation that was to bear fruit in a whole series of books—*Etruscan Roman Remains* (1892), published by Mr. Fisher Unwin, *The Legends of Florence* and *Aradia* published by Mr. [David] Nutt (1895–1896), *The Legends of Virgil* (1901) published by Mr. Eliot Stock. In his prowls about Florence he had met, by chance, a woman whom he always called Maddalena when he wrote of her, so that I hesitate to give her real name, and Maddalena she will remain. I say the meeting was by chance, but I should be more exact if I said it could not be helped, the Rye, as was once written of him, really having 'something of Burton in his delight in natural human beings other than the ordinary frock-coated, tall-hatted, high-heeled European types.'"

Leland described Maddalena as "a young woman who would have been taken for a Gypsy in England, but in whose face, in Italy, I soon learned to know the antique Etruscan, with its strange mysteries, to which was added the indefinable glance of the Witch. She was from the Romagna Toscana, born in the heart of its unsurpassingly wild and romantic scenery, amid cliffs, headlong torrents, forests, and old legendary castles. I did not gather all the facts for a long time, but gradually found that she was of a witch family, or one whose members had, from time immemorial, told fortunes, repeated ancient legends, gathered incantations and learned how to intone them, prepared enchanted medicines, philtres, or spells. As a girl, her witch grandmother, aunt, and especially her stepmother brought her up to believe in her destiny as a sorceress, and taught her in the forests, afar from human ear, to chant in strange prescribed tones, incantations or evocations to the ancient gods of Italy, under names but little changed, who are now known as *folletti, spiriti, fate* or *lari*—the *Lares* or household goblins of the ancient Etruscans."

Maddalena introduced Leland to many other Witches. In his *Memoranda* he wrote, "19 parts of 20 of the pleasure in the study of Witchcraft is the pure sense of mystery and strangeness—the delight of listening to an old fairy-tale, or of being in fairy-land. And Humour is blended with it—the vivid sense of contrast, contradiction, and,—dear delight!—of being taken out of this neat-handed five-o'clock tea Philistia of a common *comm'ondit* world."

Pioneers of Witchcraft's New Renaissance 47

In another letter to his niece, dated March 26, 1889, Florence, there is this very important passage: "A little while ago, I had given me, as a great Witch secret, a paper 'How To Make The Tree of Diana.' It is a mixture of chemicals to make a kind of foliage appear in a bottle. I had known it ever since I was a small boy, and so asked where the *witchcraft* came in? when I was told that Diana was the grand *Magia* or Queen of the Witches! Sure enough, in an Italian book 300 years old, she appears as the Queen of the Witches. Hecate is the same as Diana, the Queen of the Moon and Night. One could make no end of articles out of my witch friends."

Mary Alicia Owen, author of *Old Rabbit The Voodoo*, had sent Leland an old Indian tale from her home in St. Joseph, Missouri. He was delighted, and a correspondence ensued. While on a trip to Geneva he wrote her the following letter, dated July 22, 1889:

> Tell your Voodoo that this letter is from a great conj'ror who was intimate in Africa with the black Takroori Voodoos who conjure with Arabic books. Tell him that I know how to use *ivory rod* and *cresses* and have the *forty-nine poisons of Obeah*, and have touched the green serpent, and know more charms than any man living. Tell him that you can keep the great secret of life and death and making people *mad*, and that I recommend you to him. Tell him I have a king's stool from Dahomey and get *the root* from Dongola, and that he must teach you Voodoo and tie you a chicken's breast bone with red wool, and I will send him a *Voodoo stone* from Africa and the black book of wisdom.
>
> If you read this solemnly you will probably extract some valuable information. Tell him that

I am a Master and that he must teach you all the secrets, till I come, and that you must be given *the Great Oath.*

You are in a rich field and must cultivate it. I have recently made acquisition of a Turkish conjuror's tambourine full of strange characters, also of two mystical magical wooden images of the 14th century, about 14 inches high. There is a *great* field in Voodoo, if you don't stick at trifles and show yourself too good to poison people or break all the commandments—for it is an extremely illuminated faith and admits great freedom. Cherish your old negro as you would a grandfather, and say I will send him secrets and gifts worth having if he obeys the Master and teaches you well.

Leland's home was a treasure trove of Witch artifacts, including Witch stones with holes in them, "Odin stones," voodoo paraphernalia, roots, coins, amulets, ancient pottery, and axes. He often referred to it as his "museum." His collection of rare, ancient, and first-edition books, some gilded, would be worth a small fortune today. Yet he hated the monetary value in things, acquiring them for their curious, magical or philosophical interest. On one occasion, unable to afford a rare silver cross, he wrote, "I suffer as much from want of that cross as a poor man suffers from want of bread. What children we are with our toys."

In Florence Leland discovered all the names of the ancient Etruscan gods and goddesses, and what's more, the fact that they were known to many of the Romagna peasants. In a letter to his niece dated January, 1891, he said, "It turns out that Maddalena was *trained* as a witch. She said the other day, you can never

Pioneers of Witchcraft's New Renaissance

get to the end of all this *stregheria*—witchcraft. Her memory seems to be inexhaustible, and when anything is wanting she consults some other witch and always gets it. It is part of the education of a witch to learn endless incantations, and these I am sure were originally Etruscan. I can't prove it, but I believe I have more old Etruscan poetry than is to be found in all the remains. Maddalena has written me herself about 200 pages of this folk-lore—incantations and stories. It is a good thing that she likes to collect and write.

"*Don't give this away.* I wish you were here to help. Finding Shelta was a trifle to this."

In another letter he wrote, "I found a charming old witch the other day here—in a room full of herbs and bottles. She had a great cat who sat on a chair opposite to me, and, after I mewed to him once, never took his eyes off me. I said, 'Ah, you know me!' But the old lady only knew the common sorceries, and, when I left, said, 'You come to me to learn, but I more need a lesson from you.' Then she asked me earnestly for the Wizard's blessing, which I gave. It was really a scene for an artist, for she *looked* the witch, and as for Tom—he was actually splendid. If I had a house, I would give any money for him—I almost expected to hear him talk.

"Sad news from America! Mary Owen writes me that Alexander, the King of Voodoos, died recently."

In 1893 Count de Gubernatis founded the Italian Folk-Lore Society, a suggestion made to him by Leland four years earlier. In November of that year there was held in Rome the Italian Folk-Lore Congress. The queen herself planned to attend but backed out at the last minute because of threats on her life. Beside Leland and Count de Gubernatis, one of the main speakers was Miss Roma Lister, born in Rome of English parents, a pupil of Leland's. They both knew Witch Maddalena well, together with her friend Witch Marietta, who contributed some beautiful poems to his *Legends of Florence*.

For the last seven years of his life, Leland was in ill health. Then his lifelong devoted companion, Isabel (Fisher) Leland, died on July 9, 1902, after suffering three strokes. He wrote to his niece, "I have wept very little, and my grief is promptly met by the memory of the immediate relief from suffering which your poor aunt found in death." He also said, "It is a rest after such long suffering but, oh! how I miss the wife of more than forty years! I miss even the cares and anxiety and troubles. I must be alone for a long time."

Five months before Leland died, someone had stolen from him a box of money containing the Black Stone of the Voodoos. Somehow the Italian police found it a month before he died. "He had a great joy the other day of which I must tell you," Rev. Wood Brown wrote to his niece and biographer. "When I went in on Saturday, I found a detective in the room, and in Mr. Leland's hands was the lost Voodoo stone, over which he was laughing and crying with pleasure. It had been found on an old woman here, probably a witch, and presently the detective turned out from a bag the whole crude contents of the woman's pocket on a paper, which Mr. Leland held, to see if anything else of his was there. There was such a quantity of loose snuff that we all laughed and sneezed by turns, and then saw, to our astonishment, that beside the Voodoo stone, the woman had been carrying no less than six small magnets—no doubt a part of the stock-in-trade of her witchcraft."

His niece describes his last days as follows:

Pioneers of Witchcraft's New Renaissance

The Black Stone had worked its last spell for him, completing with a marvel the career that had begun with one, almost eighty years before.

The end was a few weeks afterwards. He had been seriously ill more than once during the autumn and winter, each illness bringing him face to face with death, each leaving him with his heart weaker. And so he had no strength to struggle when he fell ill again late in March, his heart and other troubles made the more grave by pneumonia. Dr. Paggi, who had already done much to lighten the sufferings of the last year, could not now save him. On the 20th of March 1903 with a prayer on his lips, his sister and her husband and the Rev. Wood Brown at his side, he passed on to the greatest adventure of all—the Adventure into the Unknown.

His ashes made the journey "home," for which he longed at the last, and they lie at Laurel Hill with those of the wife he missed so sorely that he could live without her but a few short months."

In Leland's *Memoirs,* he says, "John Leyland, an Englishman, now living, who is a deep and sagacious scholar, and the author of the *Antiquities of the Town of Halifax* (A very clever work), declares that for *four hundred years* there has not been a generation in which some Leland (or Leyland) of the old Bussli de Leland stock has not written a work on antiquity or allied to antiquarianism, though in one case it is a translation of Demosthenes, and in another a work on Deistical Writers. He traces the connection with his own family of Henry Leland, my ancestor, a rather prominent political Puritan character in his time, who first went to America in 1636, and acquired land which my grandfather still owned. It was very extensive."

The first complete genealogical register of an American family was that published by Judge Leland of Roxbury, Mass. It revealed that in 1847 Henry Leland had fifteen thousand descendants in America. They were members of the Massachusetts Genealogical Society. In a footnote Leland writes, "De Quincey was proud of his descent from De La Laund. I may here say that John Leyland, who is a painstaking and conscientious antiquarian and accomplished genealogist, has been much impressed with the extraordinary similarity of disposition, tastes, and pursuits which has characterised Lelands for centuries. Any stranger knowing us would think that he and I were nearly related. It is told of the manor of Leyland that during the early Middle Ages it was attempted to build a church there in a certain place, but every morning the stones were found to be removed. Finally, it was completed, but the next dawn beheld the whole edifice removed to the other spot, which a spirit-voice was heard to call (one account says that the words were found on a mystic scroll):

> Here shall itt bee,
> And here shall it stande;
> And this shall be called
> The Churche of Leyland.

All of the above relates to one of the greatest controversies in freemasonry, still unresolved: "The Leland Manuscript." In the *Encyclopedia of Freemasonry* by Albert G. Mackey, M.D., first published in 1873, there is this short biographical sketch: "LELAND, JOHN. An

Pioneers of Witchcraft's New Renaissance 53

eminent English antiquary, the chaplain of King Henry VIII, who appointed him 'King's Antiquary,' a title which he was the first and the last to bear. The king also di-directed him to search after the antiquities of England, 'and peruse the libraries of all cathedrals, abbies, priories, colleges, etc., as also all places wherein records, writings and secrets of antiquity were deposited.' Leland, accordingly, travelled over England for several years, and made many collections of manuscripts, which were afterward deposited in the Bodleian Library. He was a man of great learning and industry. He was born in London in the beginning of the sixteenth century (the exact year is uncertain), and died on the 18th of April, 1552. Anthony Wood says that he was by far the most eminent historian and antiquary ever born in England. His connection with Freemasonry arises from the manuscript containing the questions of King Henry VI, which he is said to have copied from the original."

History does repeat itself. The controversy that still exists over John Leland's "Manuscript" on freemasonry has been carried over to the manuscripts of his descendant, Charles G. Leland, notably *Aradia, or The Gospel of the Witches, Legends of Florence, and Etruscan-Roman Remains*. Are abilities inherited? Can they be transmitted via genes? Is this the result of what Carl Jung has termed the collective unconscious or a racial memory? Reincarnationists may feel that Charles Godfrey Leland was the incarnation of John Leland, thus born into this life with a predilection toward things antiquarian and occult. Others might say that he was a product of his environment and couldn't help being influenced at an early age by his associates, surroundings, and historical references to his ancestors. It is interesting to note that his first nurse was a witch. Let me quote from Leland's *Memoirs:*

> I should mention that my first nurse in life was an old Dutch woman named Van der Poel. I had not been born many days before I and my cradle were missing. There was a prompt outcry and search, and both were soon found in the garret or loft of the house. There I lay sleeping, on my breast an open Bible, with, I believe, a key and knife, at my head lighted candles, money, and a plate of salt. Nurse Van der Poel explained that it was done to secure my rising in life—by taking me up to the garret. I have since learned from a witch that the same is still done in exactly the same manner in Italy, and in Asia. She who does it must be, however, a *strega* or sorceress (my nurse was reputed to be one), and the child thus initiated will become deep in darksome lore, an adept in *occulta*, and a scholar. If I have not turned out to be all of this *in majoribus*, it was not the fault of my nurse.

The same controversy over the authenticity of the *Vangelo* (*Aradia*) is still raging over "The Leland Manuscript." When Leland's *Aradia* (and other works) was first published, the general feeling of closet critics was that his Witch-confidante Maddalena was either pulling his leg or taking him for a ride. They completely ignored the fact that he did independent investigations of her assertions and discovered that they agreed. T. C. Lethbridge, in his *Witches,* claims that Aradia is probably no older than the Middle Ages but based on beliefs that may be ancient. He laments the "political propaganda" that he feels distorts the accuracy of the book. In *Witchcraft In The Middle Ages*, Jeffrey Burton Russell, a professor of history and dean of the graduate division of the University of California, writes, "Some of the more influential, but not less worthless, of these writers include Charles Leland, whose *Aradia, or Gospel of the Witches* (London, 1899) purports to be an ancient document establishing the antiquity and high religious purpose of witchcraft—it is of course completely spurious. Alphonse Louis Constant, who wrote under the name of Eliphas Levi; Paul Pitois, who used the pseudonym Paul Christian; Arthur Edward Waite; and most recently, Gerald Gardner, whose books, including *Witchcraft Today*, are an amiable introduction to the nonsense of witchcraft as a higher religion by a man who considered himself the leader of living English witches."

The following is a complete report on "The Leland Manuscript" from the *Encyclopedia of Freemasonry* by Albert G. Mackey, M.D. From John Leland, who died in 1552, to Charles Godfrey Leland, who died in 1903, is a period of 352 years. At this writing, 1973, there have been 421 years of involvement of the Leland name and lineage in literary controversy involving two esoteric subjects which are very similar in ideas and even in some of their procedures. Freemasonry is of course much more stylized than the basically simple rites of Wicca or Wica, but both are secret societies.

> There is no one of the Old Records of Freemasonry, except, perhaps, the Charter of Cologne, that has given rise to more controversy among the

critics than the one known as the Leland Manuscript. It derives its name from the statement made in its title, which is: "Certayne questyons with answeres to the same, concernynge the mystery of maconrye; wryttene by the hande of Kynge Henry the Sicthe of the name, and faythfullye copied by me, Johan Leylande Antiquarius, by the commande of His Highnesse." It first appeared in the *Gentlemen's Magazine* for 1753 (p. 417) where it purports to be a reprint of a pamphlet published five years before at Frankfort. The title of this paper in the Gentlemen's Magazine is: "Copy of a small pamphlet, consisting of twelve pages 8vo, printed in Germany in 1748, entitled "Ein Brief von dem beruhmten Heren Johann Locke betreffend die Frey-Maurerein. So auf eine m Schreib-Tisch eines verstorbnen Bruders ist gefunden worden." That is: "A Letter of the famous Mr. John Locke relating to Freemasonry. As found in the writing-desk of a deceased brother." Hearne copied it in his *Life of Leland* (p. 67), prefacing it with the remark that "it also appears that an ancient manuscript of Leland's has long remained in the Bodleian Library, unnoticed in any account of our author yet published." Hearne speaks of it thus:

"The original is said to be in the handwriting of King Henry VI, and copied by Leland by order of His Highness (King Henry VIII). If the authenticity of this ancient monument of literature remains unquestioned, it demands particular notice in the present publication, on account of the singularity of the subject, and no less from a due regard to the royal writer, and our author, his transcriber, indefatigable in every part of literature: it will also be admitted, acknowledgement is due to the learned Mr. Locke, who, amidst the closest studies and the most strict attention to human understanding, could unbend his mind in search of this ancient treatise, which he first brought from obscurity in 1696."

The manuscript purports to be a series of questions proposed by Henry VI, and answers given by the Masons. It is accompanied by an introductory letter and a commentary by Mr. Locke, together with a glossary of the archaic words. The best account of the manuscript is contained in the letter of Locke to a nobleman, said to be the Earl of Pembroke, dated May 6, 1696, in which, after stating that he had procured a copy of it from the Bodleian Library, he adds:

"The Manuscript of which this is a copy appears to be about one hundred and sixty years old; yet (as your Lordship will observe by the title) it is itself a copy of one more ancient by about one hundred years. For the original is said to have been in the handwriting of King Henry the VI. Where that prince had it as an uncertainty; but it seems to me to be an examination (taken, perhaps, before the King) of some one of the Brotherhood of Masons, among whom he entered himself, as 'tis said, when he came out of his minority, and thenceforth put a stop to a persecution that had been raised against them."

After its first appearance in the *Gentlemen's Magazine*, it was republished in many other periodicals and books and translated into many languages. The document, if true, is invaluable as a record of freemasonry in the fifteenth century. From its first publication it has been violently attacked and just as intensely defended, with famous freemasons on both sides of the controversy. The Masons have their controversial Leland. The Old Religionists have theirs in Charles Godfrey Leland, whose *Aradia* is still being dismissed by professorial book researchers who wouldn't recognize the real thing if it hit them over the head.

MARGARET ALICE MURRAY

Margaret Alice Murray was an Egyptologist, anthropologist, and folklorist. When her *Witch Cult In Western Europe* was first published in 1921, it raised a storm of academic controversy. Her theory was that Witchcraft was a surviving remnant of an ancient religion, that it was a secret cult devoted to the pre-Christian gods, and that every king of England from the Conqueror to James I was a hidden high priest of Wicca. Her book emphasized the fact that many pagan folk beliefs and practices didn't disappear with the onslaught of Christianity but became the foundation of many Witchcraft rites.

Murray's critics pointed out that there is no record of covens as such prior to the fifteenth century, or of Sabbats, for that matter. They lament her sources, saying she ignored a great body of material, especially Continental, and seemed to fit her facts to her theories. Her work did inspire many other anthropologists, sociologists, and even psychoanalysts to do research on their own, however, and even those who started out to disprove her theories did uncover a vast body of useful material. Yet they all operate from a basically false premise. In order to prove or disprove something, one is limited by the evidence that one can uncover. Since Witchcraft has been mostly an oral tradition, the old ways and rites handed down from generation to generation, since many traditions forbade their members to write anything down as a means of self-protection and to safeguard their own secrets, and since most of them passed as Christians, Murray's debunkers only serve to debase their own positions. They can't possibly write about something they know nothing about. Witches didn't go about wearing yellow Pentagrams on their sleeves advertising their faith to all and sundry, as Jews were forced to wear yellow armbands in Nazi Germany. Those Witches who could write did so in code, often crude markings, some of them Runic, and others may have been familiar with the Ogham, but most of them did not keep a Book of Shadows as most of them do today. If discovered, it would have meant instant death!

Margaret Murray died in 1963, at the age of one hundred years. Prior to her demise she admitted to being a Witch herself. Her work has inspired countless pro and con books on Witchcraft from every conceivable viewpoint. Her value is not so much in the books that she wrote but in that she opened up a whole new field of exploration and research. One author who was influenced by her is Carlo Ginzburg, whose book *I Benandanti: Ricerche sulle Stegoneria e sui Culti Agrari tra Cinquecento e Seicento* (Turin, Italy, 1966) continues her exploration of folklore that existed in Italy during the fifteenth and sixteenth century and proves that there flourished a fertility cult devoted to the worship of Diana. One of these was called the Benandanti (the do-gooders) at Friuli. They explicitly rejected the worship of the Devil or anything like it, and often would fight pitched battles with another group, called the *strigoni*, over this matter. When the Inquisition came in, though, they themselves were called worshippers of the very thing they fought against and were murdered by the Inquisitors. Under the torturous brainwashing of the Church and its Inquisitors some of the Benandanti "confessed" to Witchcraft. Ginzburg writes, "We can surely affirm that diabolical witchcraft spread through Friuli in the shape of a deformation of an antecedent agrarian cult."

Ginzburg's book hasn't been translated into English yet. Neither has Giuseppe Bonomo's *Caccia alle Streghe: La credenza nelle streghe dal secolo xiii al six con Particolare Riferimento all'Italia* published in Palermo, Sicily, in 1959.

Jeffrey Burton Russell's *Witchcraft In The Middle Ages* is highly critical of Murray's theories. In discussing the many early researches, Russell nevertheless concedes, "Yet we are still in the debt of these scholars for directing us to a new road of approach, from which we can describe and map a terrain largely ignored by the liberals. The terrain is populated, not by the theories of philosophers or jurists, but by folk legends and tales, folk motifs in art and literature, popular feasts and festivals, the wild hunt and its hunters, secret cults, and sorcery. The folklorists' great contribution to the study of witchcraft is the recognition that the primitive elements in which beliefs were not invented either by the scholastics or the Inquisition but were handed down by folk tradition and varied from locality to locality."

Russell calls Murray's use of sources "appalling." He does concede that her work advanced important anthropological ideas, and that pagan folk practices did not die out with the coming of Christianity but became the fundamental substratum of Witchcraft. To Witches themselves, not concerned with the anthropological, intellectual, and philosophical nitpicking of scholars, Murray's important contribution was in stressing that their Horned God was in no way, shape, or form the Christian Devil. If they regret anything, it is that she stressed only the Horned God and did not explore the main deity, The Goddess. The early Christian Church, though, did recognize the Goddess, as the *Canon Episcopi,* falsely believed to be derived from the Council of Ancyra in 314 A.D., illustrates: "It is also not to be omitted that some wicked women perverted by the devil, seduced by illusions and phantasms of demons, believe and profess themselves, in the hours of the night to ride upon certain beasts with Diana, the goddess of the pagans, and an innumerable multitude of women, and in the silence of the dead of night to traverse great spaces of earth, and to obey her commands as of their mistress, and to be summoned to her service on certain nights."

Charles Godfrey Leland's *Aradia* identifies Diana with Herodias, who was believed to rule a third of the world. This probably derives from the triple aspect of the Goddess, as Hecate. In his *Etruscan Magic and Occult Remedies,* Leland cites Paulus Grillanus's *Treatise On Witches* (1547), which says that Witches "think that Diana and Herodias are true goddesses, so deeply are they involved in the error of the pagans." In Pipernus's *Treatise on the Walnut Tree of Benevento* (Naples, 1647), there are several passages calling Diana Queen of the Witches. The communities of Witches in Sicily were called Cyclopas, Lestrygonas, and Herodiades. Till this day the Witches of Naples are called *Janara* instead of the usual *Strege* (also spelled *Streghe*) throughout Italy. Ask most Napolitans why this is so, and they'll just shrug and say "They are, that's all." But this appelation is living proof that the Witches worshipped a Mother Goddess whose name was Jana. This name is just another one for Diana (Dione), the Goddess of the moon and woods, wife of Janus, which are another rustic form of Jupiter and Juno. Graves says: "But before Janus, or Dianus, or Jupiter, married Jana or Diana or Juno, and put her under subjection, he was her son, and she was the white Goddess Cardea."

In his foreword to *Witch Cult In Western Europe,* Sir Steven Runciman says, "Dr. Murray has had her critics. It was natural that occultists like Montague Summers should utterly reject theories that could not be reconciled with SATANISM OF THE DELICIOUSLY SENSATIONAL KIND they favored. To the pious, of course, it was disconcerting to find the recently canonized Joan of Arc once more facing the charge of being a witch; nor were the admirers of George Bernard Shaw very willing to accept such an interpretation of the evidence. More seriously, there were anthropologists who felt that Dr. Murray was inclined to leap at conclusions which a strict anthropological technique would not justify; and there were historians who felt that the historical background was treated a little too sketchily. Dr. Murray herself did not disarm criticism by producing later books, notably *The God Of The Witches* (1933) and, more recently, *The Divine King In England,* in which she somewhat recklessly pursued her theories further. Even many of her most fervid admirers find it difficult to believe that quite so many monarchs and statesmen as she supposed met their deaths in order to fulfill the ritualistic needs of the Dianic Cult. She has always had solid evidence to back her claims; but it has sometimes carried her into assertions which to many anthropologists and historians seem unjustified and extravagant."

Sir Steven states that the charge of extravagance cannot be hurled against her *Witch Cult In Western Europe,* even though some minor points may be open to criticism. Pennethorne Hughe said of her writings on Witchcraft, "her anthropological approach was the best thing that had happened for generations to what had become folk-lore." One wonders: Where were all the anthropologists, historians, scholars, and researchers years ago before Murray wrote her book? Leland was dismissed as a gullible romanticist. He was a folklorist and did not have Murray's academic standing. Yet he went to the people, and often the ignorant peasant is a vast repository of forgotten folklore that the learned have lost, as witness Leland's learning all the names of the ancient Etruscan Gods and Goddesses from the peasants in Italy—a feat no researcher was able to do. And why didn't some of these academically trained critics ever question why the Napolitans called witches *Janara*? Why were they willing to accept without question the confessions obtained under torture and ignore those things which refuted them? Today these same critics are combing the archives of history to prove whatever points motivate them—still insisting on there being no evidence of Witchcraft as a religion, or occasionally, when faced with irrefutable historical facts, making a few concessions—when the fact of the matter is that the *tenets of Witchcraft were not written down but handed down orally in Witch families and to those who were secretly initiated into the Old Religion.*

Another thing: There hasn't been one critic of genuine Witchcraft who has even been initiated into a coven. I'm speaking here of genuine covens and not the book-based or spurious ones. Some of their criticisms are valid and in spite of anti-Witchcraft bias serve a constructive purpose. *But none of them are based on personal experience.* They write as outsiders, objective up to a point, but nevertheless not "in." And it doesn't matter whether some Witches consider themselves the direct descendents of Nimrod or are the result of yesterday's newspaper. What is important is that they believe and practice their faith. In times past, and to a smaller degree even today, Witches themselves contributed to the general suspicion by their secretiveness. Yet, in the light of the past persecutions, who can blame them? I wonder just how many of these critics could stand up under the torture inflicted by the Inquisitional sadists and not confess to anything desired? Put a sane person into an insane asylum, and he too will go crazy. Place a simple medieval Witch into the Inquisitional madhouse and she too may begin to doubt her own beliefs. Especially when her ankles are being broken, her breasts burned off with hot irons, sulphur poured into her hair and armpits and set on fire, and all the smell of burning flesh, the so-called Black Man, the representative of the Horned God, could very easily be called the Christian "Devil." And the fact that the Goddess is seldom mentioned in Murray's archival researches may be due simply to the fact that the Inquisitors never asked about her, if they even suspected or cared; tortured Witches, or at least those accused, were only too glad to comply with what "the good Christians" wanted: confirmation of their own devilish beliefs.

Dr. Murray's account of the origins of the Order of the Garter as being directly linked to the Witch cult

Pioneers of Witchcraft's New Renaissance

has been often quoted. Briefly, the Countess of Salisbury dropped her garter during a ball, to everyone's embarrassment. Edward III gallantly came to her defense, retrieved the garter, pinned it to his own leg, and said, *"Honi soit qui mal y pense."* Roughly translated, this means "Evil to him who thinks it." Edward founded a knightly order called the Order of the Garter, consisting of twelve knights for himself and twelve for the Prince of Wales. The King's mantle was powdered over with 168 garters, and with the one worn on his leg, that made a total of 169—which is thirteen times thirteen. Pennethorne Hughes says, "This ingenious implication is slightly invalidated by the fact that garters had been in fashion for several years. However, Miss Murray's suggestion is attractive, and shoes with cleft toes, bitterly condemned by the church, were, perhaps not entirely by coincidence, in vogue at much the same period." His point—that a leader of the coven, the Christian-named "Devil," dressed in this way—was only natural for the time. He does not comment further on the magical number thirteen.

This is just too much for coincidence. Furthermore, an exact description of the Countess of Salisbury's garter has not been given. Today, as in olden times, many Witch High Priestesses wear a special kind of garter; the color and fabric differ in the many different traditions. When a High Priestess has other covens stemming from her own, a buckle is added to her garter for each new one and she becomes known as a Witch Queen. The title of royalty applies only to those covens stemming from hers and does not imply jurisdiction over others of a different tradition.

The word *Sabbat* was derived from the French word *s'esbettre,* which means "to frolic," Dr. Murray declared.

Montague Summers quotes what he considers to be "scholarly authorities" who are "agreed to derive it from the debased Bacchanalia" tracing it to the Phrygian God Sabazius, "who was generally regarded as the patron of licentiousness and worshipped with frantic debaucheries." Others claim that it has nothing to do with the number seven or the Jewish Sabbath. Personally, I believe it does stem from the latter, especially when one realizes how the Jews were held in contempt by the Church, and all sorts of debased and degenerate rituals were attributed to them. For centuries the Church called Jews "the killers of Christ." The twelfth synod of Toledo (January 9–25, 681) passed laws against both the Jews and Magicians, and specifically condemns the Jewish Sabbat (Sabbath in Latin in *Sabbaticus*). Later in the Middle Ages the revulsion against Jews and Witches culminated in their calling the Witch meetings Sabbats. Jew, heretic, and Witch were synonymous in the prejudiced ecclesiastical mind. A modern example of this kind of thinking is the white supremacist who considers all nonwhite people "niggers." And of course he is always willing to believe the worst. Regardless of the origin of Sabbat, it is used today by Witches and is the correct term for their major holidays.

Murray wrote, "As it is certain that the so-called 'Devil' was a human being, sometimes disguised and sometimes not, the instances in which these persons can be identified are worth investigating. In most cases these are usually men, and the names often given, but it is only in the case of the Devil of North Berwick that the man in question is of any historic importance; the others are simply private individuals of little or no note." She does admit that it occasionally was a woman. Whether called the Devil, Grand Master, Magister,

Magus, or Leader of the Coven, in the cases which were not the result of torture or delusion, it indicates that the Witch High Priest wore the mask and horns of an animal as representative of the Horned God. In some cases the High Priestess may have adorned male garments and antlered head-dress in the absence of the High Priest. And it is more than possible that in those covens which actually practised a fertility rite an artificial phallus could have been used by the leader of either sex. His usually being described as "black" may refer either to a dye used on his skin or the clothes that he wore.

The story of Francis, later Earl of Bothwell, the suspicion that he was the leader of a coven of Witches, especially in the plot on King James's life, and his implication in this by the confession of John Fian, who later retracted it though viciously tortured, is worth reading in Murray's *Witch Cult In Western Europe*. In a footnote, she writes, "It is perhaps significant that the confession of John Fian, and the trials of both Barbara Napier and of Bothwell himself for witchcraft, have disappeared from the Justiciary records."

Dr. Murray accurately summed up the true feelings of Witches, past and present, in her introduction to Gerald Gardner's *Witchcraft Today:* "Dr. Gardner has shown in his book how much of the so-called '*witchcraft*' is descended from ancient rituals; and has nothing to do with spell-casting and other evil practices, but is the sincere expression of that feeling towards God which is expressed, perhaps more decorously though not more sincerely, by modern Christianity in church services. But the processional dances of the drunken Bacchantes, the wild prancings round the Holy Sepulchre as recorded by Maundrell at the end of the seventeenth century, the jumping dance of the medieval 'witches,' the solemn *zikr* of the Egyptian peasant, the whirling of the dancing dervishes, all have their origin in the desire to be 'Nearer, my God, to Thee,' and to show by their actions that intense gratitude which the worshippers find themselves incapable of expressing in words."

Anthropologist T. C. Lethbridge, after discussing Leland's *Aradia* in his book *Witches*, says, "Turning to Dr. Margaret Murray's publications, we find that, since much of her information comes from the reports of trials, from which the witches seldom escaped with their lives, the picture is somewhat different from that given by the Italian 'gospel.' There is little, if any, trace of a goddess; although modern members of the cult admit that their chief deity is female, though they may not mention her name. The evidence from the trials ranges in time from the fourteenth to the seventeenth centuries and therefore can be assumed to be more or less contemporary with the 'gospel.' Since the witches may not mention her name now, the reason why the goddess is not found in the trial accounts is presumably the same. Magic was the main purpose of Aradia's teaching and since the telling of a person's name to a magician gives him a hold over that person, it was clearly important for the witches not to mention the goddess' name to their enemies. This must be the explanation of the discrepancy."

GERALD B. GARDNER

Called everything from "The Grand Old Man of Witchcraft" by his followers to a "dirty old man" by his ex-followers and detractors, Gerald B. Gardner's life and character was very different from that of Charles Godfrey Leland. The latter approached Witchcraft as an involved scholar. Gardner's approach was that of the hard-sell salesman. Flamboyant and at times fraudulent, his personality was more suited to that of the ceremonial magician than to that of a Witch. The simple, unpretentious rites of Wicca were a bit too tame for his tastes and ambitions. For this reason he broke away from the coven of "Old Dorothy" Clutterbuck and formed his own without having ever obtained the second or third degree entitling him to do this.

Since the facts of Gardner's life have been published many times before, only a brief sketch will be given here. One of his disciples, Jack L. Bracelin, wrote a book called *Gerald Gardner: Witch,* published in England. Naturally it was biased in Gardner's favor, the more lurid details completely omitted. This is typical of all those who call themselves "Gardnerians" who write about him. In the 1972 issue of *The Witches Almanac,* there is an article on him by Raymond Buckland, in which he says, "In 1949 Gerald was permitted —rather grudgingly, by his High Priestess, Dorothy—to publish a book called *High Magic's Aid.* This was written (very entertainingly) as a novel, but gave a truer picture of witchcraft than had been shown until that time." Buckland of course is a "Gardnerian." For an entirely opposite view, Francis King, in his *Ritual Magic in England,* said, "In the late 'forties Gardner wrote, under the pseudonym of *Scire,* a long and almost unreadable novel called *High Magic's Aid* which dealt with magic and witchcraft in mediaeval England. The book seems to have been a resounding flop—five years later I saw the publisher's shelves still groaning under the weight of the unsold copies—but it did arouse a little interest among those inclined to such subjects, and Gardner soon acquired a few followers." In a footnote to the above, King writes, "While the book appeared under the imprint of Michael Houghton, Ltd., an occult bookseller of Museum Street in London, I believe that Gardner himself met the costs of production."

In the same *Witches Almanac* article, Buckland made this fantastic statement: "The coven which Gerald originally joined was a Celtic group (as in Christianity there are various denominations, so in witchcraft). In later years Gerald went through the rituals and corrected them, where errors had crept in. He brought them back to what was probably their original form. Later followers of these rituals then became known as 'Gardnerians.' Witches after Gerald. A better name might, perhaps, have been 'Purists.' However, since the name does honor Gerald's work, it is a good one."

The above self-serving statement is fantastic because Gardnerian rites are a conglomeration of Celtic ritual, ceremonial magic, and bits and pieces from here and there, including passages in their Book of Shadows lifted directly from Leland's *Aradia,* and others written by Aleister Crowley, whom Gardner paid—all of them strung together by Gardner's own personal quirks and fantasies. The only "Witches" who would concur with the above paragraph are those who have been initiated into Gardnerian covens. Their agreement is based on their own biased feelings. Francis King wrote a devastating critique of Gardner citing the Crowley-written rituals and "at about the same time, either forged, or procured to be forged, the so-called *Book of Shadows,* alledgedly a sixteenth-century witches rulebook, but betraying its modern origins in every line of its unsatisfactory pastiche of Elizabethan English."

What is most interesting is that the dust jacket of Francis King's book has a paragraph of praise by Buckland—so he obviously knew the facts when he wrote the *Witches Almanac* article. The constant use of Gardner's first name, Gerald, implies that Buckland met or knew him personally. This is disputed by some of his ex-members. As to that "purist" remark, let me quote Francis King once more: "Unfortunately, Gardner was a sado-masochist with both a taste for flagellation and marked voyeuristic tendencies. Heavy scourging was therefore incorporated into most of his rituals and what Gardner called the 'Great Rite' was sexual intercourse between the High Priest and High Priestess while surrounded by the rest of the coven."

Here are a few biographical facts about Gardner. He was born on June 13, 1884, of Scottish parentage. His father was a justice of the peace, his mother a member of the Browning Society. He had four brothers. Because of an asthmatic condition, his family sent him with an Irish nurse to live in Europe. He also lived briefly in the Canary Islands. In 1900 Gardner began his first job on a tea plantation in Ceylon. He became friendly with the natives and took various notes on everything that he saw. This habit was continued later when he worked in Borneo. He worked at various jobs, including customs inspector and government inspector of opium establishments.

In Malaya he became friendly with the Saki and eventually wrote a book about their wavy-bladed knife, *Kris and Other Malay Weapons*. His anthropological interests culminated in his discovering the true site of the ancient city of Singapura, now Singapore. After travels to Saigon, Indochina, and China, he retired on a pension in 1936 and returned to England. He made contact with a number of occult groups, one of them in Christchurch, Hampshire, who claimed to be Witches. Just after the start of World War II he was initiated into this coven. He claimed Grizell Gairdener as an ancestress. She was burned as a witch in Newborough, Scotland, in 1640.

Gardner's early life provides a valuable insight into his character. His father, William Robert Gardner, was a rich lumber merchant. One of his odd habits was to take off his clothes when it rained and sit on them until the shower was over. His Irish nurse was a buxom belle who liked men and whisky in equal proportion. Though basically good-hearted, she tended to beat Gerald whenever he interfered with her own pursuits. Her nickname was "Com." They traveled together, Gerald collecting knives and "Com" collecting amorous knaves. She finally married a wealthy tea planter from Ceylon when Gerald was sixteen, and both of them sailed for Colombo. That was the beginning of his Eastern interests which later turned to Western occultism, including spiritualism. While visiting England in 1927 he married his wife Donna, convinced that it was prophesied by spirit.

Undoubtedly influenced by his nude-oriented father, Gardner later became a full-fledged nudist. In March, 1939, he joined the Folk Lore Society in Britain, contributed to its journal *Folklore*, and remained a member until his death. About this time he joined another group located in Christchurch, in the New Forest where he first met "Old Dorothy", often called "Doffo," Clutterbuck. She convinced him that Witch-

Pioneers of Witchcraft's New Renaissance

craft was the survival of a pre-Christian fertility cult, the Old Religion. She initiated him as a first-degree witch.

Gardner's membership in the Folk Lore Society, the very same one founded by Charles Godfrey Leland years before, was often an embarrassment to other members. Christina Cole, author of *Witchcraft in England* and other books, was then Editor of the *Folklore Journal*. When he died, it did not carry his obituary. Miss Cole wrote the following letter to *Man, Myth and Magic*:

> "Dr. Gardner had a very curious personality. It did not inspire confidence—at least not in me, nor in a number of people interested in witchcraft and kindred matters. His theories were in themselves somewhat peculiar. I remember a meeting when the composition of the Council for the following year was discussed, and the question was raised as to whether his presence on our Council was really advantageous to the Society. Nothing was done about it, and his name was allowed to go forward as before, but the doubt was clearly felt and expressed."

One of the little-known facts about Gardner is that he and Jack L. Bracelin, his biographer and beneficiary, cofounded the nudist colony at St. Alban's. This biography is really a hagiography. In America Raymond Buckland has taken up where Jack Bracelin left off. There is no record that Gardner ever got any kind of university degree, honorary or otherwise. In his vagabond travels with his nanny Com he had little time for formal education. He even taught himself to read, a fact he admitted to Bracelin. In the late fifties he probably secured a mail-order degree in the United States. The Folk Lore Society membership list for November, 1950, credits him with the degrees of M.A. and Ph.D. The *Authors and Writers Who's Who,* 1963, lists him with a Ph.D. and D.Litt., yet the next sentence says he was "privately" educated.

In my book *Black Magic, Satanism, and Voodoo,* I wrote, "Shortly afterwards Gardner was initiated into this coven of hereditary witches. He wasted no time in acquiring all the accoutrements of witchcraft, including such extraneous items as having his body tattooed with daggers, dragons, snakes and cabalistic signs. On Lammas Day 1950 he participated with 'Old Dorothy' in a coalition of covens called 'Operation Cone Of Power' to stop Hitler's armies from invading England."

To paraphrase the Christians, the Goddess works her wonders in many mysterious ways. Gardner, despite his personality and sexual idiosyncrasies, captured the public's imagination. Whatever criticisms can be leveled at him, one of them is not insincerity. He was deeply devoted to the Craft even though he may have incorporated some elements compatible to his own needs. But then again, as a pagan it wasn't necessary that he wear the halo of Christian saints (most of whom were "sinners" far surpassing Gardner before they became sanctified). And it's ludicrous for certain people today to try to deify him. He was a man. He was a Witch. He had his faults. He had his virtues. In his zeal Gardner tended to either overlook or be ignorant of certain older Witchcraft traditions. He was called to task for this in the now defunct British *Pentagram: A Witchcraft Review* in its March, 1965, issue. In an article entitled "Ancients and Moderns" by Taliesin, he discussed Gardner's ignorance of the use of the hallucinogenic mushroom, the *amanita muscaria,* by olden Witches:

> I once asked the late Gerald Gardner what he knew of this mushroom, so deeply embedded in the myths of Britain that no illustrator of children's fairy stories—even today—fails to include it somewhere. He answered that he knew nothing of it and did not himself believe that it ever formed a part of the Old Religion. This proves just how well the secret had been kept all this time, because Gardner was completely wrong. I have not only seen a late fifteenth-century recipe for a sort of tea brewed from the mushroom, but I have ritually drunk it. The revulsion against so-called "toadstools" gives us the clue to all this. Many of these fungi are very edible indeed, but countrymen will not touch them. This almost certainly points to a time when certain of these fungi were taboo because of their sacred quality, i.e., they were for eating on religious occasions only—and then probably only by the priestesses and priests. Robert Graves suggests that the English reluctance to eat horsemeat could come from a similar race memory. The "unclean" animals and birds of the Bible are almost certainly the same sort of thing.

On October 3, 1964, about fifty people attended the *Pentagram* dinner in London in conjunction with the Witchcraft Research Association, including Gerard Noel, editor-founder, and Mrs. Doreen Valiente, author of the excellent book *Where Witchcraft Lives.* In her opening address, Mrs. Valiente paid tribute to Gardner, "for the great contribution he made to the renewal of interest in the survival of the old Craft of the Wise. I do not by any means agree with all that Gerald Gardner said or did; but I recognize his great qualities of heart and mind, as did all who knew him. He was a personality and character, and we shall remember him with affection.

"The name of Gerald Gardner is so much associated with Witchcraft in the present day, that he has even been paid the back-handed compliment of having the allegation made that he invented it! I think I need only say in this connection that if people will believe that, they will believe anything.

"*Pentagram* is now contacting surviving traditions from covens which have never been in any way connected with Gardner. In fact, it is becoming increasingly clear that the old Craft has survived in fragments all over the British Isles. Naturally, these different groups, which have lost touch with each other over the centuries of persecution, have to a certain extent grown apart. Each has its own version of the tradition, in its own words; and each has its own ideas of practice and ritual. It is proving a tremendously exciting project, to compare these different fragments of tradition, and see wherein they complement each other, and where they may differ."

The controversy between the Gardnerians and traditional or hereditary Witches in England has carried over to the United States and is still raging. However, recently we had an Ecumenical Council of Crafters in New York representing five traditions—Continental, Sicilian, Welsh Traditionalists, Pagans, and Gardnerians —and we found out that we could all enjoy and respect each other's differences, that we genuinely liked one another, and that our common interests and goals far exceeded our differences. As in England and elsewhere, it was discovered that the newer Witches were the ones who were the most rigid, who lacked fluidity, and who were the first to attack others not of their own tradition. One of the persons who liked to think of himself as part of an "in" group was suspected of never having been initiated, especially since he tried to get a Gardnerian initiation and was turned down by the High Priestess.

Robert Graves has said, "Apparently the equal division of the sexes in modern covens is Dr. Gardner's contribution to the craft; for Dr. Murray shows that although every medieval coven had its maiden as assistant to the Chief, men were in the majority." He has also written, "But the Two Horned did not dance naked; nor did any medieval British Witches. The modern cult has borrowed its nudism either from the Far East or from Germany—where souvenir shops in the Harz mountains have long been selling figurines of naked young Brocken Hexen astride brooms." Graves was undoubtedly unfamiliar with the passage in *Aradia, the Gospel of the Witches* by Leland that Gardner and others may have used as sanction for their nude worship.

Gerald Gardner was Witchcraft's most prolific proselytizer, but he was not a prophet, as the following written by him in 1954 will show: "I think we must say goodbye to the witch. The cult is doomed, I am afraid, partly because of modern conditions, housing shortage, the smallness of modern families, and chiefly by education. The modern child is not interested. He knows witches are all bunk."

The Craft itself is split by many schisms. The distrust of centuries spills over into other Old Religion traditions. Crafters themselves are a highly suspicious lot, and not without reason. Unfortunately, this has tended to create more ill feeling and splits even among those who are genuine in their faith. But there are rank opportunists who run mail-order schools granting Instant Witch certificates, whose courses are a conglomeration of excerpts from the Christian grimoires and their own masturbatory fantasies. One such person recently wrote a spurious book saying that all female Witches carry a handmade dildo, that an adolescent boy has his penis circumcised by the mother and a girl has her hymen broken by the father using an artificial phallus. These people advertised their Witchcraft courses in the sex columns of the Los Angeles Free Press. They are and were always considered to be nothing more than perverse Christians by others in the Craft. They sold out for thirty pieces of silver and capitalized on the sex-crazed fantasies of those who have a malicious or repressed reason for wanting to believe the worst about Witches. Their book makes no distinction between the various traditions of Wicca, but presents its garbage as something true of all Witches. Despite their pretensions and their protests, on the psychic plane they are nothing more than common criminals and will be Karmically prosecuted. Their book of course will be avidly quoted by the fundamentalist fascists—a false book giving false ammunition to the Biblical bigots. And not once in this literary piece of trash do they ever mention the Goddess—only the God. Because of the blatant deception, a petition denouncing them was signed by many Witches, representing different branches of the Craft. Furthermore, some of their students planned to file a suit against them for "using the mails to defraud." For once Witches will welcome any court suits this entails, since the evidence is on their side.

In the past the Craft has been sexually oriented, but this must be viewed in the light of its being a fertility religion, one in which the sexual act was sacred, without the guilt-ridden, dirty-minded, obsessive character given to it by puritanism. The Great Rite used in many traditions, mostly symbolically today, consists of the High Priest's inserting the athame into the chalice held by the High Priestess, saying, "As the knife is to the man, so the cup is to the woman. Joined together they are one in truth." And in the past Crafters did fornicate in the fields in the belief that this would insure an abundant harvest. Today, with modern agricultural methods, there is no need for this.

Another Witchcraft tool which Gardner employed was the scourge. Most modern Gardnerians use it only symbolically. Covens have to be constantly on guard against attracting bad elements: sadomasochists or those interested in the Craft solely for sexual reasons. These, though, usually eliminate themselves when they discover that the Old Religion is precisely that: a religion. Nowadays the emphasis is on fertile minds. After all, any submoron with the necessary biological equipment can conceive. Though Witchcraft has been called "low magic," that doesn't mean that its practitioners are of low mentality or morality.

Gerald B. Gardner's books are must reading for all those sincerely interested in the Craft. Despite his faults, he singlehandedly brought the Old Religion to the forefront of public attention—something viewed with horror by its more traditional diehards—and this has been both good and bad. Since his demise, thousands of books have been written on Witchcraft, most of them worthless, but the truth has also gotten through and inspired others to do research on their own.

3

The Mother of Us All

"In the beginning God made man," the Bible says. And of course Eve was fashioned out of Adam's rib! Witches and Pagans today are apt to paraphrase the Biblical version into "In the beginning Goddess made woman." The male Holy Trinity of the Catholic Church was preceded by a feminine triad. In Witchcraft many worship the Triple Aspect of the Goddess, which can be equated to the three phases of the moon—waxing, full, and waning—or to the young maiden, the mother, and the crone. Aristotle, in the fourth century B.C., in his *On The Heavens*, wrote, "All things are three, and thrice is all: and let us use this number in the worship of the gods; for as the Pythagoreans say, everything and all things are bounded by threes, for the end, the middle, and the beginning have this number in everything, and these compose the number in the Trinity."

Egyptian religion arranged its deities in threes:

The Mother of Us All

Osiris, Isis, and Horus; Amen, Mut, and Khonsu; and Khnum, Satis, and Anukis. The Hindus had as their Holy Trinity Brahman, Siva, and Vishnu. The Assyrian Trinity consisted of Asshur (Assur and Asher), Anu, and Ea, sometimes given as Anu, Bel, and Ea. In Greece they had Om (On), Dionysius (Bacchus), and Hades, or Zeus, Poseidon, and Hades. The Norse trinity consisted of Odin, Thor, and Friga. In Arabia the divine triad was composed of Al-Lat, Al-Uzzah, and Manah. The Phoenician Trinity was that of Belus (the sun), Urania (the earth), and Adonis (love).

Students of Witchcraft, the Old Religion, should familiarize themselves with *The White Goddess* by Robert Graves and *The Great Mother* by Erich Neumann. Most books written on "witchcraft" for popular consumption rarely, if ever, mention that the supreme deity of the Witches is a Goddess. Among the recommended books which do cover this are *Witches* by T. C. Lethbridge, *Witchcraft Today* and *The Meaning of Witchcraft* by Gerald B. Gardner, *Aradia, The Gospel of the Witches* by C. G. Leland, *Witchcraft: The Sixth Sense* by Justine Glass, and *The Witches Speak* by Patricia Crowther. Most people attracted to the Craft of the Wise have been reared as Judeo-Christians. Even if they came from nonreligious homes, the fact remains that they have been conditioned to hearing and reading the constant mention of the male God. Even our currency has printed on it "In God We Trust."

The religions of the Great Mother covered the world in the past, and she has been known by innumerable names, depending upon national origin. Some of her names are Aphrodite, Astarte, Ashtart, Artemis, Bridget, Bride, Diana, Cailleach, Persephone or Proserpina, Demeter or Ceres, Libera, Hecate, Luna, Cybele, Isis, Habondia, Andred, Herodias, Bellona, Arianrhod, Ariadne, Fortuna, Hel, Friga—the list is endless. Most major religions, especially those of the West, have dropped the worship of the Mother Goddess. The Catholic Church reinstituted her in the deification of the Blessed Virgin Mary, yet their Holy Trinity is made up of Father, Son, and Holy Ghost—male. The title "Mother of God" was first used by the theologians of Alexandria, Egypt, which was the center of Isis-worship towards the close of the third century. When Christianity began to spread rapidly in the fourth century, that title was usurped and applied to Mary, mother of Jesus. In A.D. 400 Epiphanius denounced the women of Thrace, Arabia, and elsewhere, for worshipping Mary as a Goddess. But in A.D. 430 Proclus preached a sermon hailing Mary as divine and a mediator between God and Man. Nestorius objected, preferring to regard her the same way as the early Christians did: a chosen channel for a divine birth but herself mortal. Then in 431 Cyril of Alexandria gave a passionate defense of Mary's divinity, insisting that she filled the void in human affections left vacant by Isis and Diana of Artemis (or Ephesus). Nestorius was deposed, to the great delight of the people. Henceforth Mary was the Supreme Queen of Heaven, the Mother of God, the Christian incarnation of all of the other Goddesses that preceded her.

Long before the sixth century, stories began to be told about Mary's miraculous ascension into heaven, so that the Church finally inaugurated the feast of the Assumption, one of its major holy days. It was abolished by the Church of England during the Reformation, but gradually made a comeback via Anglo-Catholics who celebrate it on August 13—most interesting, as this date was the great feast of Diana or Artemis, often identified with Isis. Not only Isis was identified with the crescent moon; so were Selene and Venus and Aphrodite. Countless depictions of the Christian Mary show her with crescents. Isis was Goddess of the Sea and of seamen. Later the title of *stella maris,* "star of the sea," was given to Mary. There is a carving of Isis with a ship in her hand, on an ivory panel, which was inserted into the side of the pulpit in the Cathedral of Aix, where it exists to this day. And in the church of Ursula at Cologne a statue of Isis was adopted in the Middle Ages as one of the capitals of the pillars.

Isis was also identified with the Goddesses Astarte, Ashtoreth, or Ashtoroth, all known as "the queen of heaven," to whom women made offerings. Even today the Christian women of Paphos, Cyprus, make such offerings to the Christian Madonna in the ruins of an ancient temple of Astarte.

Antioch was one of the earliest seats of Christianity. There was celebrated the death and resurrection of the god Tammuz or Adonis each year. The name Adonis itself simply means "The Lord." This faith exerted a great influence on Jewish thought, the prophet Ezekiel (Jerome, Epistle 58, *ad Paulinum*) rebuked the women of Jerusalem for weeping for the dead god Tammuz at the gate of his temple. Even the site selected as the birthplace of Jesus by the early Christians (the exact site was unknown) was a shrine to the pagan god Tammuz, a fact which horrified St. Jerome when he discovered it. This shows how Tammuz and Adonis became confused in most people's minds with Jesus Christ. Their legends are exactly like those of Jesus: They suffered a cruel death, descended into the underworld, were resurrected, and then ascended into heaven. The body was made into an effigy which was bathed and anointed. The following day, the last one of the Tammuz-Adonis festival, there were great rejoicings with shouts of "the Lord is risen." The festival was timed to coincide with the appearance of the planet Venus as the Morning Star. Even today, in certain parts of Greece and Sicily this Adonis festival retains its pagan past though ostensibly in honor of Jesus Christ.

Another contributory influence to early Christianity was the worship of the God Attis and the Goddess Cybele. Attis, the Good Shepherd, was the son of the Great Mother, the Virgin Nana, Cybele, who supposedly conceived him without sexual union with a man. As a young man Attis mutilated himself via self-castration and bled to death at the foot of his sacred pine tree. In Rome his festival of death and resurrection was held from March 22 to 25. Later the Catholic Church pronounced March 25 as the anniversary of the Lord's passion in those countries where Attis-worship was most prevalent: Phrygia, Gaul, Italy, and other countries. The church of St. Peter, on Vatican Hill, stands on the exact spot where the worshippers of Attis and Cybele celebrated their rites. The rites themselves often consisted of the new initiates' castrating themselves, throwing the bloody sex organs onto the altar, then running through the streets until given shelter and garments. Afterwards most of these eunuch priests dressed in female attire.

The legend of Osiris and Isis is that they were brother and sister, as well as husband and wife. Osiris was murdered, his coffined body thrown into the Nile. Shortly afterwards Isis gave birth to Horus. Osiris's coffin was washed up on the Syrian coast, where it lodged in a tree trunk. It was cut down and made into a palace-pillar at Byblos, where Isis later found it. She removed the coffin, mourned, placed it in a temple, and took the body of Osiris back to Egypt. There his body was found by evil powers who tore it to pieces, which were later put back together again, whereupon the god Osiris rose from the dead. Later he returned to the underworld, reigning as King of the Dead. His son Horus, now grown, reigned on earth. The feast of the resurrection of Osiris ranged from October 21 to November 8, depending upon what calendar was used. Later this same feast was Christianized into All Souls Day, celebrated November 1, wherein lamps and candles are burned all night, in the same way the devotees of Isis-Osiris did. The feast of All Saints is held on October 31— Samhaim or Halloween. This is another instance in which the Church incorporated a pagan feast-day as one of their own. Unable to suppress this widespread pagan custom, the Church recognized it officially in A.D. 998. The feast of All Saints was recognized by the Church in 835, and it's obvious that there are overlappings of the two days.

Isis-worship was introduced into Rome in the first century B.C. Sulla founded a college of Isis there. There were temples to her at Pompeii, Malcesina on Lake Garda, and later many other places all over Western Europe. There even was a Temple of Isis in Southwark, London. Her worship survived up to the fifth century A.D., making it one of the last of the pagan faiths to maintain itself under the Christian onslaught. Of especial interest to Witches is the fact that one of the temples to Isis was founded in the city well-known for its Witches' Sabbats: Benevento, Italy, mentioned in *Aradia.* Till this day a famous liquor is made there, called *La Strega,* featuring witches with broomsticks on its label. The name itself became a synonym for free love when during the joyous sabbats everyone grabbed a partner and made love.

C. G. Leland, in his "Comments On The Foregoing Texts" in *Aradia,* writes, "The strange and mystical chapter 'How Diana made the Stars and the Rain' is the same given in my *Legends of Florence,* but much enlarged, or developed to a cosmogonic-mythological sketch. And here a reflection occurs which is perhaps the most remarkable which all this Witch Evangel suggests. In all other Scriptures of all races, it is the male, Jehovah, Buddha, or Brahmin, who creates the universe; in Witch Sorcery it is the female who is the primitive principle. Whenever in history there is a period of radical intellectual rebellion against long-established conservatism, hierarchy, and the like, there is always an effort to regard Woman as the fully equal, which means the superior sex. Thus in the extraordinary war of conflicting elements, strange schools of sorcery, Neo-Platonism, Cabala, Heretic Christianity, Gnosticism, Persian Magism and Dualism, with the remains of old Greek and Egyptian theologies in the third and fourth centuries at Alexandria, and in the House of Light of Cairo in the ninth, the equality of Woman was a prominent doctrine. It was Sophia or Helena, the enfranchised, who was then the true Christ who was to save mankind."

Elsewhere in the same chapter, Leland says, "It is in studying the epochs when woman has made herself prominent and influential that we learn what the capacities of the female sex truly are. Among these, that of Witchcraft as it truly was—not as it is generally quite misunderstood—is as deeply interesting as any other. For the *Witch*—laying aside all question as to magic or its nonexistence—was once a real factor or great power in rebellious social life, and to this very day —as most novels bear witness—it is recognised that there is something uncanny, mysterious and incomprehensible in woman, which neither she herself nor man can explain: 'For every woman is a Witch at heart.'" Then he adds, "To all who are interested in this subject of woman's influence and capacity, this Evangel of the Witches will be of value as showing that there have been strange thinkers who regarded creation as feminine development or parthenogenesis from which the masculine principle was born. Lucifer, or Light, lay hidden in the darkness of *Diana*, as heat is hidden in ice. But the regenerator or Messiah of this strange doctrine is a woman—ARADIA, though the two, mother and daughter, are confused or reflected in the different tales, even as *Jahveh* is confused with *Elohim*."

In his book *Ancient Sex Worship*, Sha Rocco writes, "Mother Earth is a legitimate expression, only of the most general type. Religious genius gave the female quality to earth with a special meaning. When once the idea obtained that our world was *feminine*, it was easy to induce the faithful to believe that natural chasms were typical of that part which characterizes women. As at birth the new being emerges from the mother, so it was supposed that emergence from a terrestrial cleft was equivalent to a new birth. In direct proportion to the resemblance between the sign and the thing signified was the sacredness of the chink, and the amount of virtue which was imparted by passing through it. From natural chasms being considered holy, the veneration for apertures in stones, as being equally symbolical, was a natural transition. Holes, such as we refer to, are still to be seen in those structures which are called Druidical, both in the British Islands and in India. It is impossible to say when these first arose; it is certain that they survive in India to this day. We recognize the existence of the emblem among the Jews in Isaiah vi, 5, where the wicked among the Jews were described as 'inflaming themselves with idols under every green tree, and slaying the children in the valleys under the clefts of the rocks.' It is possible that the 'hole in the wall' (Ezek. viii, 7) had a similar signification. In modern Rome, in the vestibule of the church close to the Temple of Vesta, I have seen a large *perforated stone,* in the hole of which the ancient Romans are said to have placed their hands when they swore a solemn oath, in imitation, or, rather, a counterpart, of Abraham swearing his servant upon his thigh—that is, the male organ. Higgins dwells upon these holes and says: 'These stones are so placed as to have a hole under them, through which devotees passed for religious purposes. There is one of the same kind in Ireland, called St. Declau's Stone. In the mass of rocks at Bramham Crags there is a place made for the devotees to pass through. We read in the accounts of Hindostan that there is a very celebrated place in Upper India, to which immense numbers of pilgrims go, to pass through a place in the mountains called the Cow's Belly.' In the island of Bombay, at Malabar Hill, there is a rock upon the surface of which there is a natural crevice which communicates with a cavity opening below. This place is used by the Gentoos as a purification of their sins, which they say is affected by their going in at the opening below and emerging at the cavity above . . . 'born again.' The ceremony is in such high repute in the neighboring countries that the famous Conajee Angria ventured by stealth, one night, upon the Island, on purpose to perform the ceremony, and got off undiscovered. The early Christians gave them a bad name, as if from envy: they called these holes 'Cunni Dia boli' (*Anacalypsis*, p. 346)."

Besides the fertility aspects of the Mother Goddess, there is the concept of parthenogenesis, wherein eggs from virgin females are developed without male spermatozoa. The word itself derives from the Greek *parthenos*, "maiden," plus *genesis*, whose root means "to be born." Thus, virgin birth. Sir E. A. Wallis Budge, in his *The Gods of the Egyptians*, says, "The statements of Greek writers, taken together with the evidence derived from the hieroglyphic texts, prove that in very early times Net was the personification of the eternal female principle of life which was self-sustaining and self-existent and was secret and unknown and all-pervading; the more material thinkers, whilst admitting that she brought forth her son Ra without the aid of a husband, were unable to divorce from their minds the idea that a male germ was necessary for this production, and finding it impossible to derive it from a power or being external to the goddess, assumed that she herself provided not only the substance which was to form the body of Ra but also the male germ which fecundated it. Thus Net was the prototype of parthenogenesis."

Another belief was that the ancient Gods and Goddesses were androgynous, possessing the sex organs of both sexes, thus able to reproduce themselves. There are countless carvings, engravings, paintings, and statues depicting the ancient deities as hermaphroditic. Such figures have been discovered dating from the neolithic age in Spain, Yugoslavia, and elsewhere. A clay hermaphroditic idol was found in Yugoslavia and dated from the Bronze Age. The word itself is derived from Greek mythology: Hermaphroditus was a son of Hermes and Aphrodite, who while bathing became joined in one body with a nymph. There are many images of "bearded ladies," including the Goddesses Diana and Isis as two examples; The Goddess Neith with a fully erect male organ, as was the Nordic Venus, Friga (or Freya); Venus, Aphrodite, Baal, Mithras, Zeus, Adonis, Dionysius, and countless other deities were described and portrayed as androgynous.

In my book *Black Magic, Satanism, and Voodoo*, I wrote, "In the oldest records of India, China, Babylon, Egypt and Greece the first gods are represented as bisexual. The Greeks often depicted Apollo as both male and female. Bacchus was similarly described. Proclus, commenting on the Timaeus of Plato, says: 'Jupiter (Zeus) is a man, Jupiter is an immortal maid.' Citing further Orphic verse it mentions that all things are contained 'in the womb of Jupiter.'

"In Cyprus, Venus, depicted as Aphrodite, sometimes had a beard! Diana or Artemis had characteristics of both sexes. Orpheus taught that since the gods possessed the generative powers to create all things, they were, of necessity, both male and female. A Babylonian tradition described the first men as having one body and two heads, one male and one female. A Hindu scholar drew a figure of Brahma, during the act of creation, making him bisexual. The Babylonian God Tammuz was consecrated a Qedesha (Kedesha) which is a sacred prostitute (I Kings 19:24). Jahveh, the Hebrew God, is made up of *Jah* masculine and the second syllable from havvah, feminine. It comes from Yaw or Yah, the name of a prehistoric male-female moon-god venerated by South Arabian Semitic tribes.

The Jews tagged on the feminine root making it Yahweh or Jahwah. The Christian Bible spells it as Jehovah because of an error in translation. The Books of Job and Isaiah depict Jahwah as having the characteristics of both sexes."

Witchcraft, the Old Religion, was and is concerned with fertility, but it is not restricted to that alone. Today with fertility pills, modern forms of agricultural methods, and the trend towards smaller families, this aspect has been elevated and the stress is on fertile minds. Those groups who insist on heterosexuality as a requirement for admittance into a coven cannot claim ancient precedence, since so many of the pagan religions had male prostitutes in their temples. And the eunuch priests, most notably of Cybele, would be disqualified. Then too, since the Craft is supposed to be basically nondogmatic, this would be a contradiction of its own beliefs. Those Witchcraft sects who do discriminate against homosexuals are usually the newer ones headed by the sexually insecure, or those who use the Craft as a ritual means of fornication. And to stress the fertility aspects is to discriminate against not only homosexuals but also all women who have had tubal ligations or hysterectomies, and all men who have undergone vasectomies. This sexual-fertility stress is hypocritical, since most married Witches don't have more than two or three children. All those who use birth control are, in effect, acting against fertility. Today there is no need to fornicate in the fields in order to make the crops grow. Scientific methods have taken care of that. The only reason why any coven should bar a qualified homosexual from admittance would be because it practices "The Great Rite," sexual union between the High Priestess and the High Priest brought up to Third Degree. Or vice versa. Yet even in this, most leave such a decision up to the people involved, and most would choose the symbolic Great Rite—the inserting of the consecrated athame into the sacred chalice. I've often wondered just how dedicated some of these few-in-number antihomosexual High Priests would be if the Goddess appeared to them and requested that they make the great sacrifice: self-castration.

What was held as an ancient religious belief, the feminine principle ruling the universe, is now taking on scientific validation. In a past issue of *Green Egg*, the publication of the Church of All Worlds, its High Priest Tim Zell published a long article entitled "Theagenesis: The Birth Of The Goddess," showing how all life evolved from a single mother cell. He writes:

> The Paleo-Pagans, diversified though they were, held among them certain common viewpoints. Among these were: veneration of an Earth-Mother Goddess; animism and pantheism; identification with a sacred region; seasonal celebration; love, respect, awe and veneration for Nature and Her mysteries; sensuality and sexuality in worship; magic and myth; and a sense of Man being a microcosm corresponding to the macrocosm of all Nature. These insights, however, were largely intuitive, as science had not yet progressed to the point of being able to provide objective validation for what must have seemed, to outsiders, to be mere superstition. Twentieth-century Neo-Paganism, however, has applied itself and the science of its era to that validation, and has discovered astounding implications.

The Mother of Us All

A single cell develops physically into a human being by a process of continuous division and subdivision into the myriads of cells eventually required to make up an adult body, groups of cells specializing to become the various organs and tissues needed for full functioning of the organism. Now, when a cell reproduces, the parent cell does not remain intact, but actually *becomes* the two new daughter cells. Since the same protoplasm is present in the daughter cells as was in the parent, the two daughter cells still comprise but a single organism; one living being. The original cell ceases to exist in that form, but its *life* goes on in the continuous evolution of the growing organism. Thus, the billions of cells of the adult human body continue to comprise a single living organism, even though different cells may be highly specialized, and some may even be mobile enough to travel independently around in the collective body. No matter how complex the final form of the adult organism, no matter how diversified its component cells, the same thread of life of the original cell, the same protoplasm, continues in every cell in the body. Since the sex cells are also included in this ultimate diversification of a single original cell, the act of reproduction carries this same thread on in the offspring, combined with the equivalent thread of protoplasm from the other parent. Thus your children, while spatially distinct from you, are in fact as much a part of your growing, evolving organism as your blood cells (which can easily be extracted and survive independently of your collective body) or tissue cells (which can also be extracted and grown in independent cultures).

Your children are still "you"—your own living protoplasm continues on in their cellularly-diversified bodies. And in your children's children for all generations to come. All the cells in all your descendants will still comprise but ONE LIVING BEING.

Tracing our evolution back two billion years, through mammals, reptiles, amphibians, fish, and so on, we eventually wind up with ONE SINGLE CELL that was the ANCESTOR OF ALL LIFE ON EARTH. Even though there were undoubtedly many proto-cells formed in the early seas, the first one to develop the capacity to reproduce would have quickly consumed all the available free proteins and amino acids floating in the sea, effectively preventing the development of any competitors. Cell reproduction occurs at a fantastic geometrical rate, which, unchecked, would result in all the planet being buried beneath the progeny of a single cell within months. Obviously, what checked this fantastic reproductive potential was a limited food supply, which would have included any not-yet formed or newly-formed competitive cells. But when this cell reproduced itself, and continued to do so for eons, some of its daughter cells mutating and evolving into new forms, it still, as in the human body, continued to comprise but a SINGLE total organism. When a cell divides and subdivides, NO MATTER HOW OFTEN, the same cellular material, the same protoplasm, the same life, passes into the daughter cells, and the granddaughter cells and the great-granddaughter cells, FOREVER. No matter how often or for how long this subdivision goes on, the aggregate total of the new cells continues to comprise ONE SINGLE LIVING ORGANISM.

Zell says that all life on earth contains only L-amino acids and that we are literally all one. He calls the planetary organism "Terrebia." He delves into many other technical details, too extensive to quote here. He believes that Teilhard de Chardin, in his book *The Phenomenon of Man* was correct in his vision of an emerging planetary consciousness—what he termed the "Omega Man," or what Carlton Berenda called "the first coming of God," in his *New Genesis*. Then Zell defines divinity as follows:

> Divinity is the highest level of aware consciousness accessible to each living being, manifesting itself in the self-actualization of that being. Thus we can truly say, "All that grows is God." Divinity is a cat being fully feline (as all cats are!), grass being grassy, and Man being fully Human. Collective Divinity emerges when a number of people (a culture or society) share enough values, beliefs and aspects of a common life-style that they conceptualize a tribal God or Goddess, which takes on the character (and the gender) of the dominant elements of that culture. Thus the masculine God of the Western Monotheists (Jews, Christians, Moslems) may be seen to have arisen out of the values, ideals and principles of a nomadic, patriarchal culture; the ancient Hebrews. Matriarchal agrarian cultures, on the other hand, personified their values of fertility, sensuality, peace and the arts in the conceptualization of Goddesses. As small tribes coalesced into states and nations, their Gods and Goddesses battled for supremacy through their respective devotees. In some circumstances, various tribal divinities were joined peaceably into a polytheistic pantheon, being ranked in status as

their followers' respective influences determined. In other circumstances, one particularly fanatic tribe was able to completely dominate others and eliminate their own deities, elevating its God to the status of a solitary ruler over all creation, and enforcing His worship upon the people. However, no matter to what rank a single tribal deity may be exalted by its followers, it still could be no other than a tribal divinity, existing only as an embodiment of the values of that tribe. "Gods are only as strong as those who believe in them think they are." (ALLEY OOP). When the planetary consciousness of Terrebia awakens, it too will be Divinity—but on an entirely new level: the emergent deity Berenda postulates in *The New Genesis*. Indeed, even though yet unawakened, the embryonic slumbering subconscious mind of Terrebia is experienced intuitively by us all, and has been referred to instinctively by us as Mother Earth, Mother Nature (The Goddess, The Lady). Indeed, this intuitive conceptualization of feminine gender for our planetary Divinity is scientifically valid, for biologically unisexual organisms (such as amoeba and hydra) are always considered female; in the act of reproduction they are referred to as mothers and their offspring as daughters.

Zell concludes his "Theagenesis" with: "Thus we find that 'God' is in reality Goddess, and that our Paleo-Pagan ancestors had an intuitive understanding of what we are now able to prove scientifically. Thus too do we expose the logical absurdity of a concept of cosmic Divinity in the masculine gender. These few pages, however, have only been the briefest of introductions to the implications of a discovery so vast that its impact on the world's thinking will ultimately surpass the impact of the discovery of the Heliocentric structure of the solar system. This discovery, which we shall explore in more detail in future articles, is the discovery that the entire Biosphere of the earth comprises a single living organism. Blessed Be."

Worship of the Mother Goddess is worldwide. However, in 1902 a contractor discovered the now world-famous Hypogeum of Hal Saflini in Malta. This is a huge underground temple hewn out of solid rock, a neolithic marvel. Zammit, the curator of the Valetta Museum in Malta, has dated it at 3000 B.C. The May, 1920, *National Geographic* magazine presented an article "Malta: The Halting Place of Nations" by William Arthur Griffith, in which he described the Hypogeum's *"Oracle"* as follows:

> . . . at about the level of a man's mouth is a hemispherical hole in the wall about two feet in diameter. Here it was noticed only a few months ago that any word spoken into this place was magnified a hundredfold and audible throughout the entire underground structure. A curved projection is specially carved out of the back of the cave near this hole and acts as a sounding board, showing that the designers had a good knowledge of sound-wave motion. The impression upon the credulous can be imagined when the oracle spoke and the words came thundering forth through the dark and mysterious places with terrifying impressiveness.

Malta is a seventeen-and-a-half-mile-long island only sixty miles away from Sicily. Both islands have not only played a great part in world history, but are believed to have been settled by peoples of the same racial stock. The *strege* undergrounds of both islands have long maintained strong ties. In the Temple of Hagar Kim, many fascinating relics were found, including a four-sided pillar with a flat round top, possibly a sacramental altar. Each side had pittings at the edges while the centers had carvings of a many-leafed plant growing out of a vase, remarkably similar to the Tree of Life. "The most remarkable find consisted of seven stone carved figures of steatopygous females," Griffith writes, "some draped with plaited skirts and others apparently nude. Possibly they were originally painted entirely red, as red ochre paint is still largely visible. . . . One figure has a sort of pigtail behind, which might also have served as a handle to permit the image to be carried in a procession. None of them had heads, although sockets were found into which detachable heads could be fixed.

"These figures suggest that they were worshipped as the Mother Giver of Life. They are sometimes described as the Seven Cabiri of the Phoenicians, to which nation all Maltese antiquities and even the race itself were until recently ascribed. Subsequent discoveries have proved beyond doubt, however, that these images were of neolithic age."

All of Malta is covered by an underground of temples stretching from one end of the island to the other. Many feature stone slabs with flat tops, weighing tons each, very similar to those of England's Stonehenge. Many were phallic symbols containing a huge stone cone and two huge stone balls. Some of these temples had a "holy of holies" with a sacrificial altar. The walls at the temple of Tarxien contained carvings in bold relief of a bull, a sow, and a second bull facing the first. These carvings are considered to be some of the earliest known of the type. Underneath the altar was found two large bull horns, suggesting that this animal may have been worshipped in Malta the same as the Minotaur was worshipped in Crete. Like the British and French varieties, these stone altars were known as *menhirs* and *dolmens*. Griffith writes, "There appears little doubt but that the early Maltese belonged to the same stock as the Iberians of Spain, the Basques of the Pyrenees, the Gauls of France, and the small, dark men of Cornwall, South Wales, and Ireland."

The early inhabitants of Malta, as determined by examination of the skeletons of the polished-stone age, seem to have had the same bodily structure as the early Egyptians who spread westward to the Mediterranean islands of Malta, Sicily, Sardinia, and Spain. And like Sicily, Malta at one time or another has been conquered or inhabited by Carthaginians, Phoenicians, Greeks, Romans, Vandals, Arabs, Normans, Spaniards, and Turks. In A.D. 60 St. Paul landed on Malta, called Melita in the Bible (Acts of the Apostles). The fantastic prehistoric remains on Malta indicates a past civilization so remote that it predates the age of hieroglyphics and even oral tradition. There are traces of wells and pits all over the island. Black tufa stone-rubbers from Sicily have been found, as well as obsidian from the Greek islands. In a cave near Mnaidra was found the remains of a peculiar kind of elephant called *Elephans mnaidrensis*.

In one underground chamber of the Hypogeum was found the bones of over 33,000 persons, all in great disarray, along with broken pottery and figures of a Goddess. Opinions vary as to whether this was a burial ground, an underground temple dedicated to the spirits who had left this world, or a sacred college of priests and priestesses where they were initiated into the mysteries. Some of the female figures were made of alabaster. One was of a woman with small head and large abdomen, obviously a fertility figure, lying on her side asleep on a four-legged couch. There were also ax-shaped pendants made of jade and polished stone, again a possible link with the ax-worshippers of Crete. Two objects were obviously fish. Even in those days the fish was considered an emblem of the Giver of Life, and the Christian adoption of it as their symbol during the Catacomb days of Rome was a survival of this older belief. Of especial interest to old Religionists is the black polished plate which had flint-drawn figures of several large horned bulls, identical to those carved on the Stone Age Temple of Tarxien.

Perhaps the best proof of Mother Goddess worship in prehistoric Malta is the following statement by author Griffith: "In connection with the worship of Matriarchy, it is curious to note that the Maltese language contains no word for 'father' which conveys the idea of a head of a family. Their word 'missier' literally means 'instrument of generation' and suggests the time when descent was reckoned maternally rather than paternally.'"

Let me repeat that most significant phrase: *The Maltese language contains no word for father.* To my knowledge the above statement cannot be made for any other Mother Goddess race or by modern Pagans or Witches who revere the Feminine Principle or the Female Deity. The Maltese language itself is basically Phoenician, with mixtures of Latin and Arabic. But because it has been part of the British Commonwealth, English is taught in the schools.

In the August, 1940, issue of *National Geographic* magazine, Richard Walter's "Wanderers Awheel In Malta," in describing the underground maze of temples, tunnels, and catacombs, tells why the Maltese Government closed it to the public: "On a sight-seeing trip, comparable to a nature study tour in our own schools, a number of elementary school children and their teachers descended into the tunnelled maze and did not return.

"For weeks mothers declared that they had heard wailing and screaming from underground. But numerous excavations and searching parties brought no trace of the lost souls. After three weeks they were finally given up for dead."

Many Sicilian and Maltese Witches say that the true secrets of Hal Saflini have not been discovered and that those teachers and children are not dead but are now part of a living race of people still surviving in their underground homes, still worshipping the ancient deities, and protected from discovery by various booby-traps that could initiate landslides should explorers get too close. The teachers and young children who were lost insured the propagation of their race—new blood mingling with old—providing a stronger stock for their Maltese underground matriarchy.

Most books written on Witchcraft and the Old Religion in recent years have dealt primarily with European, and especially British-based, Witchcraft. The Magick of the Mediterranean is generally glossed over. Recently one Craft publication had an article by one of those *nouveau* Witches which was chauvinist and racist, his initiation having been performed by someone belonging to a branch of the Craft considered "fringe" by older hereditary and traditional groups. He wrote, "I would say accept separate traditions for northern and southern beliefs. I find the former to be more spiritual than the latter—and no slight is intended for either group. The Mediterranean witch, and I base this solely on the literature, has an element of violence and vengeance which I have yet to encounter in the northern or Celtic Craft as I know it. Why this is, if indeed it is true, I am not quite certain.

"Research and speculation, however, leads me to conclude the Mediterranean witch is a degenerate form of a more spiritual forebear. Lacking the present upsurge of popularity and its resultant surge of recruits the northern witch could become the same. The southern witch mainly works alone. The northern works still in the coven—be it large or small. One maintains the group or Craft discipline of integrity, the other is left to the spiritual character of an individual."

The person who wrote this, under a Craft pseudonym, is in the Air Force and served in Vietnam, whence he wrote letters home which were blatantly racist, to the effect "Let's kill the gooks and get home," whose Book of Shadows contains direct passages from *Aradia,* an Italian—Mediterranean—"Gospel of Witches," and whose statement totally neglects all those Teutonic War Gods. This person knows absolutely nothing about Southern or Mediterranean Witches, has never attended one of their Sabbats, and of course his vague references to the "literature" doesn't specify his sources. These two paragraphs indicate the technique of insecure new Witches (if they are that), especially a certain group whose members are notorious for lying out of both sides of their mouths, who make unsupportable charges "in confidence," and who are guilty of doing that of which they accuse others. Instead of attacking openly, they make a pretense of literary criticism and indulge in character assassination and blatant deception as a cover-up for their own inadequacies. This person and his cohorts deeply resent me for publicising the spying activities of another Air Force "Witch" on the Peace Movement and for treating them with the contempt that they deserve. And despite all their pretentions and childish cloak-and-dagger games, I let them all know that I knew their real identities. Their tradition is of course "skyclad," (or nude) and they use the scourge—symbolically of course—and if the truth were known about his *nouveau* tradition the perverse use of "degenerate" for Mediterranean and "more spiritual" for the "Northern" Witches would be enough to send him (and them) back to the Judeo-Christianity from which they're refugees anyway.

As a Sicilian Witch, a Mediterranean Mago, I know that the above statement is not one motivated by the Mother Goddess, whether of the North or South, but by a patriarchal male chauvinism and racism which is contrary to Old Religion ethics. I consider such people traitors to both our Mother Goddess and the Horned God.

4

Holy Horns and Halos

The Christian-depicted Devil with horns and hoofs, and added tail, is their degenerate Satanized version of the God Pan, whose existence is much older than the other Greek Gods. In Rome they called him Faunus (sometimes Silvanus), the God of flora and fauna. He ruled the forests, fields, and farms. He was the God of Hunting, supreme ruler of all the animals, horned and otherwise. The Celtic Gauls called him Cernunnos (which means "The Horned") who ruled the underworld, a place where souls resided until they were reincarnated on earth again. Underneath the Cathedral of Notre Dame in Paris, there is an altar dedicated to Cernunnos featuring a Horned God with his inscribed name. Despite the Latinized name, evidence indicates that he was the supreme deity of Gaul. The altar was once a sacred site on which was His temple. As usual the Catholic Church usurped this site for its own religious edifice.

The most oft-quoted reference to the Horned God is that of the cave painting in the Caverne des Trois Frères (Cave of the Three Brothers) in Ariege. It depicts a man dressed in stag skins and wearing antlers on his head. The face is bearded. This stag-man is drawn on the upper part of the cave wall. Below him are drawn other animal figures. He's the dominant one and seems to be performing some sort of ceremony. The painting is placed in a position where it cannot be seen unless one is directly beneath it. This indicates that it was a sacred representation and drawn in such a way as to hide it from the uninitiated. This painting is dated as going back to the late paleolithic period.

Rational historians claim that the first Gods were personifications of the sun and moon. Psalm 84:11 says, "The Lord God is a sun and shield." The sun was considered the Father, the moon the Mother, especially in ancient and Latin races. However, Germans say *die Sonne* (feminine) and *der Mond* (masculine). The Australian aborigines also consider the sun feminine and the moon masculine. From ancient paganism to modern Christianity the symbolism of the sun and moon has been preserved in the wheel-cross, the crown, and the halo. The Blessed Virgin Mary was preceded by other celestial Goddesses usually depicted with a crescent moon, often worn in a way to denote miniature horns. It is often called the Horned Moon. These Goddesses include Ishtar, Isis, Artemis, Diana, and Hera-Io. The Egyptian God Osiris was represented by the bulls Apis and Mnevis, while Isis in the form of Hathor was the short-horned cow. In Greece they depicted the God Zeus with horns, and in Rome Jupiter was horned. Ramman, the Chaldean God, was often depicted with two pairs of horns with the symbols of the sun and moon over his head. In his hands he holds an ax and a thunderbolt. This symbolizes his double power. From this we can see how the triple crown given to Catholic Popes evolved.

Though the crescent is usually ascribed to women today, the Egyptian Gods Thoth and Chonsu wore the crescent as a crest. Chnemu, called "The Molder," is shown with a pronounced ram's head, on each side of which were cow horns. The halo on pictures of saints is nothing but a carryover of the sun and full moon. The crowns of kings, emperors, queens, and ecclesiastics continue the symbolism (though its origin may be unknown to the wearers). The various spikes or spokes on crowns represent the sun's rays. The spear-shaped rays on the crowns of pictures of the Madonna carry the analogy further. In the Vatican Museum there is a statue of Juno Sospita wearing the skin and horns of a goat on her head. This is in the same position as those on pictures of the American Indian Chiefs Mahtawopah and the Blackfoot Petohpeekiss, which represent bison horns. There are also many horned Muses, and Mercury is often shown with wings formed like horns on his head. In one case he wears the crescent between the wings. Bacchus or Dionysus is also shown horned; Horace called him *bicorniger* which means two-horned. One of the most famous (some think infamous) is Michelangelo's statue of Moses wearing horns.

The horned Moses has been a controversial issue for centuries. Yet in the Bible, Deuteronomy 33:17, referring to Moses, it says, "His glory is like the firstling of his bullock, and his horns like the horns of unicorns." Horns were universally recognized as a symbol of authority and power. In the book *Horns of Honour* by Frederick Thomas Elworthy, he writes, "The Israelites were, of course, quite familiar with horns upon the heads of the gods of Egypt, and fresh from the land of bondage they would readily believe that their great lawgiver had become divine, that he had miraculously received the mark of divinity and of kingly power. The belief that Moses actually descended with solid horns upon his head was devoutly held, and has continued to be believed down to the Middle Ages. Even later, the learned Grotius says that the god Mnevis (always represented with horns) who was worshipped among the Egyptians, is believed to be no other than Moses himself. Mnevis was the sacred bull of Heliopolis, as Apis was that of Memphis. Spannheim lends his great authority to this by quoting Grotius, and supports it by adding that Aben Esdra himself believed the same. He says, too, that St. Jerome held fast the belief in actual horns on the head of Moses, and he (Spannheim) makes his remarks seem all the more probable, in establishing what was the belief of the Israelites, by the production of numerous coins bearing horned heads both bearded and beardless. A Greek one of Agrina in Sicily has a horned head, which may be either male or female, but looks most like a woman; another of Gela has an undoubted female face."

Robert Graves alludes to both the horned Moses and Alexander the Great in his book *The White Goddess*. Alexander didn't sack the Temple of Jerusalem, explaining that he bowed down before the Tetragrammaton on the High Priest's golden frontlet as the symbol of the God he represented whom he saw in a dream. This convinced him that Jehovah was on his side and would lead him to victory. Graves writes, "The high priest then further encouraged Alexander by showing him the prophecy in the *Book of Daniel* which promised him the dominion of the East; and he went up to the Temple, sacrificed to Jehovah and made a generous peace-treaty with the Jewish nation. The prophecy referred to Alexander as the 'two-horned King' and he subsequently pictured himself on his coins with two horns. He appears in the *Koran* as Dhul Karnain, 'the two-horned.' Moses also was 'two-horned,' and in the Arabian legend 'El Hidr, the ever-young prophet,' a former Sun-hero of Sinai, befriended both Moses and Alexander 'at the meeting place of two seas.' To the learned Gwion, therefore, a banner borne before Alexander was equally a banner borne before Moses; and St. Jerome, or his Jewish mentors, had already made a poetic identification of Alexander's horns with those of Moses."

Elsewhere Graves describes New Grange, built of stones, 50,000 of them, as "A Bronze Age Sepulchral practice in honor of the White Goddess, which may account in part for the legends of Kings housed after death in glass castles." These were covered with white quartz pebbles. In it was found two full skeletons lying beside a central altar, stags' antlers, bones, and nothing else. This cave was rediscovered in 1699. Graves writes, "The antlers at New Grange were probably part of the sacred king's head-dress, like the antlers worn by the Gaulish god Cernunnos, and the horns of Moses, and those of Dionysus and King Alexander shown on coins."

In Elworthy's *Horns of Honour* he says, "The frontispiece to the writer's copy of Delrio's *De Magia*, 1603, shows Moses with conspicuous horns, when with Aaron he is standing before the Almighty, and also in eight other of the scenes representing the plagues of Egypt; in every case before the Exodus, and long before his descent from the Mount. Torreblanca's *De Magia* has a frontispiece showing the same scenes though differently treated. In each, Moses has horns distinctly portrayed. These curious anachronisms do but support the evidence of the belief in actual concrete horns."

The Salii, the priests of Mars in ancient Rome "Flamines Martiales" wore a single horn on their heads, called an *apex*. It is similar to those worn on the helmets of German soldiers up to World War I. The Salii made sure that their caps never fell to the ground, as this was a sign of dishonor. One Sulpitius was "defrocked" as a priest because his fell to the ground while performing his service. Alexander the Great was called the "two-horned," and E. Wallis-Budge in his *Life of Alexander The Great* (1896), says, "the most natural explanation of this title is obtained by assuming that one of the attributes of Amen-Ra has been applied to Alexander. As the legend makes Amen-Ra his father this assumption is a fair one. Darius III addressed Alexander: 'Behold it has reached me that thou, the Two-Horned, hast assumed the sovereignty over Greece without my order. . . . I will march out against thee."

Long before Alexander's time, helmets with two horns were worn by soldiers, a custom continued by the Romans, Celts, Italians, and others up to the fourteenth century. These horned helmets can be found in various museums today, including the British Museum. The ancient Etruscans, Belgi, and Saxons all placed horns on their helmets, as tokens of victory or defiance. The *panache* of heraldry is a crest which in the days of chivalry became a synonym for horns. The plumed hats or crests of heraldry are but symbolic or substitutional horns. In the Italian *tromba* (trumpet) as another name for horn, when used to describe a musical instrument. It also means cornucopia and ram's horn. From this we can see how the "ear of Jupiter" (often shown with ram's horns) supplies the air (literally and musically) and his power over that element. Elworthy writes, "the horn placed on the side of his head becomes a conventional symbol of power over that element. At the same time it denotes his chief attributes—the sun in his might, as Aries the progenitor, and also as the bull Apis. We must never forget that this very surname, *Serapis,* perpetuates this Egyptian faith in a triune god, first brought to Rome by the Ptolemies, for it is but the contraction of the compound Osiris-Apis."

From the rays of the sun, the calathus, the corn measure, and horns—symbols of ancient pagan divinities and their power—have come the modern crowns of kings and queens or those worn by the Catholic hierarchy. From the wreath worn by Diana of Ephesus to those worn by winners in modern Olympian games, the symbolic sign of power, of victory, even of illumination, remains. The Romans had a number of special crowns worn for different occasions. The most coveted was the *corona obsidionalis,* made from the poorest materials such as grass, wild flowers and weeds, reserved for the general who liberated a captured city. The second highest crown was called the *corona civica,* made up of oak leaves, given to a soldier who had saved a citizen's life. Third, the *corona rostrata* and the *corona navalis,* given to those who had successfully invaded a hostile ship. There was also a *corona miralis* given to the one who had first climbed the wall of a besieged city. The *corona castrensis* was given to the first soldier who first gained entry into an enemy's camp. The *corona triumphalis* was given to the triumphant general, while the *corona ovalis* (myrtle) was

Holy Horns and Halos 111

the reward of the successful commander. The *corona oleagina* (the olive) was presented to brave soldiers, from which our modern military decoration is derived.

The pagan priests wore the *corona sacerdotalis*. The *corona funebris* is placed on a bier of a dead person and not worn. From this is derived our modern funeral wreathes and flowers. There were other wreaths for nuptials and celebrations.

In old illustrations of the crowns worn by the kings of Israel, they all feature a pronounced fringe of upright spikes. These are common in many old paintings of the Italian royalty, often consisting of a single band of metal from which long spikes curve over the head. Numerous paintings of the Catholic Madonna have fanciful or modified spiked crowns. The fleur de lis is one example. Crowns that feature a cross and an orb are traced to the ancient *crux ansata*, the ankh, the symbol of life to Egyptians, the astronomical sign of Venus and considered an amulet against evil. The button on these crowns, later evolved into larger orbs surmounted by a cross, is nothing but a throwback to the calathus worn on the head of Jupiter-Serapis.

Feathers and plumes are another modified emblem of horns. They are seen on the head of Osiris in old pictures and on the crest of the Prince of Wales and featured on numerous family crests. In the Cathedral of San Gennaro, Naples, the famous saint whose blood is supposed to liquefy, where there were near riots recently when the Pope spoke against the festivities, one of the side chapels belonging to the Minutoli family, contains two sides of the lower walls painted with almost life-sized knights, twenty-one in all; twelve of them are wearing double-horned helmets. During the reign of the Aragonese lords of Naples, there were many tournaments. Each knight presented himself at the sound of the *tromba*. The wearing of the *trombe* on a knight's head was the sign of victory, and it was either two horns or none at all. Thus in the Cathedral wall paintings those who have none on their helmets were obviously vanquished in the tournaments. Those who lack them represent graphically the Italian proverb *"Tornare con le trombe nel sacco, o scornato"* which means "To come back with the horns in a bag, or deprived of horns"—in modern parlance, to come home empty-handed, unsuccessful, defeated.

An historian quoting the above and unfamiliar with its origins would not be able to make any sense out of it. An example of how origins can be lost and words change their meaning is in the word *scorn*. The Italian *scornare* means to dehorn or deprive of horns. The Italian noun *scorno* has the same meaning today as our own English word scorn: disgrace, shame, or contempt. The old French word *escorné* is translated as "shame, disgrace, contempt, defaced, ruined." Modern Frenchmen use the word écorné now to describe contemptuously someone who is impotent. Those who become *escorné* in marriage are called *cornards!* One who is dishonored is literally dis-horned! Though the honor of horns is still kept in regal crowns, through a process of idea and semantic revolution it also acquired one of disgrace, undoubtedly affected by the Christian Church's devil-propaganda.

By the sixteenth century the ancient respect paid to horns as a symbol of highest honor degenerated into one of disgrace. Shakespeare was obviously well versed in both, as the following from his *As You Like It* (IV, 2) indicates:

Jacques. Which is he that killed the deer?
1st Lord. Sir, it was I.
Jacques. Let's present him to the Duke, like a Roman conqueror; and it would do well to set the deer's horns upon his head for a branch of victory. Have you no song, forester, for this purpose?
2nd Lord. Yes, sir.
Jacques. Sing it; 'tis no matter how it be in tune, so it make noise enough.
"What shall he have that killed the deer?
His leather skin, and horns to wear.
Take thou no scorn, to wear the horn;
It was a crest ere thou wast born:
    Thy father's father wore it,
    And thy father bore it.
All:
The horn, the horn, the lusty horn,
Is not a thing to laugh and scorn."

Shakespeare reveals his astute historical insight in his *Measure for Measure* (II, 4:16) when he writes:

Let's write good angell on the devill's horne;
  tis not the devill's crest.

In Captain Bourke's *Scatologic Rites of all Nations,* he writes, "The horns of honor of the deities worshipped by women who were ordered by their husbands to become religious prostitutes were transferred to the husband: what had been the outward sign of extreme devotion and self-abnegation was turned into ridicule and opprobrium." From their former exalted station of honor, the wearing of horns became a symbol of disgrace. Even in Italy and Sicily today the obscene gesture with the forefinger is well known as is the *mano cornuta* made in a special manner—the highest insult to another. Other races use it too, but since gesture is so much a part of the Italian-Sicilian heritage, the meaning is far more deadly to them. The *jettatura*, made with the forefinger and the little finger to form horns, is used as a protection against the *mal'occhio* (evil eye). Another such gesture is the touching of one's genitals (for which it is said the late Italian dictator Mussolini was notorious). It's not difficult to see the phallic association between genitals and horns. In fact many Italian buildings had horns on them, engraved or built right into the structure, and of course the "lucky horseshoe" hung over doorways the world over is just another symbolic depiction of the protective horns. The word *corno* in the Italian vernacular is a synonym for penis, and the many charms and amulets come under the collective term *un corno*. While on this subject, many Christians would be horrified to learn that the popular pastry called "hot crossed buns" originally were made with the image of a phallus baked into them. The Christian priests made the populace substitute the cross.

Unbeknownst to both priests and peasants, the substitutional cross was another ancient phallic symbol long before Christianity. It was found on the borders of the Nile: An upright piece of wood tied to a horizontal beam indicated the height of the flood waters. This Nile-o-meter formed a cross. If the waters failed to rise to a certain height during the planting season, this meant poor or no crops. From feast to famine, the cross was revered as a symbol of life and regeneration, or feared as one of decay and death. The Egyptian *ankh* represents both the male and female genitals. The cross itself is a primitive form of the male genitals: the triad, three in one. In prehistoric times tribes observed that most male animals had horns and undoubtedly associated this as a sign of potency and power with their own genitals. The slang term "horny," used today, needs no explanation.

In the museum of Taranto, Southern Italy, there are many terra cotta sculptured heads, medallions, and ornaments excavated there showing the heads of various Goddesses with horns, some unmistakably Medusa. They all have Pan-pointed ears. Often the horns are symbolically substituted by the placement of wings or snakes so arranged as to indicate horns. The symbol of Sicily was the *fylfot,* a figure containing the head of Medusa with three legs, wings for ears, and two snakes forming horns on the head. Ancient Sicily was called *Trinacria.* This emblem is also called the *triskelion* or *triquetra.* It was adopted by Agathocles as the badge of Sicily in 317 B.C. It is interesting to note that it was also later adopted by the Isle of Man but without the Medusa head, consisting mainly of three legs. The Manx arms are borne by many old English families, as Elworthy points out in his *Evil Eye,* "and are said to have been brought to England by Crusaders returning *via* Sicily."

"The intimate connection between the protective and dignifying quality of horns," Elworthy says, "as a decoration is well illustrated by a piece of ritual which has lasted from early times down to these scientific, matter-of-fact days. In the Naples Museum is a great Assyrian bas-relief of a priest wearing a mitre, on which the two points are shaped into unmistakable horns, and it is of course well known that the two points of a

Christian bishop's mitre, taken from the traditional headdress of the Jewish high priest, typify horns, and thereby convert that headdress into a badge of power and dignity. In a Missal at Bologna of 1517 is another bearded bishop wearing a mitre, on which a very distinct white horn, painted upon a darker background, springs from the forehead to the top of the mitre, where it forms the point.

"Perhaps not everybody is aware that the words still used in setting the mitre upon the head of a newly-consecrated bishop in the Roman Church are: 'We set on the head of this Bishop, O Lord, Thy champion, the helmet of defence and of salvation, that with comely face and with his head armed with the horns of either Testament he may appear terrible to the gainsayers of the truth, and may become their vigorous assailant, through the abundant gift of Thy grace, who didst make the face of Thy servant Moses to shine after familiar converse with Thee, and didst adorn it with the resplendent horns of Thy brightness and Thy truthm and commandedst the mitre to be set on the head of Aaron, Thy high priest, Etc." (Copies of this in Latin and in translation can be found in *The Order Consecration of a Bishop Elect* with the *imprimatur* of H. Card. Vaughn, p. 14, Burns and Oates, 1893)

In the light of the above, Bible students will find the following of interest: "He is my shield, and the horn of my salvation" (2 Samuel 22:3). "And hath raised up an horn of salvation for us" (Zacharias in Luke 1:69). "My buckler, and the horn of my salvation" (Psalm 18:2).

From horn to helmut of salvation is one jump, as the following demonstrates: "For he put an helmet of salvation upon his head" (Isaiah 59:17). "Take the hel-

Holy Horns and Halos

met of salvation" (Ephesians 6:17). "And for an helmet, the hope of salvation" (1 Thessalonians 5:8).

T. C. Lethbridge, in his excellent book *Witches: The Investigation of an Ancient Religion*, discusses the hills of Wandlebury known to thousands of Cambridge people as the Gogs or Gogmagogs, in which archaeological excavations unearthed three figurines, two male and one female on a horse. The latter was a big surprise; Lethbridge writes, "A female figure was, however, unknown and uncontemplated. Yet we should have thought of it, for Irish story is full of great goddesses and tales of them survive in both English and Scottish folk-lore. Archaeologists, however, are largely governed by what they can see and handle. The idea had grown up that hill figures were always men, or horses; a female figure was abominable. Well, there she is with her horse and three years of work went into her uncovering."

This figure turned out to be an Artemis with several breasts, probably four. Lethbridge continues, "She points to them with her right hand. In the left, like Brigid, she holds a disc, which is probably intended to represent the 'Apple of Life.' Above her head, a great horned shape has not been excavated, but is probably a moon symbol. The association with the horse is most important, for not only is the horse what we might have expected, if the builders of Wandlebury were Iceni, the horse-folk; but the horse is a symbol of the sun. It seems that the picture as a whole is intended to suggest that the sun is about to mate with the moon. Lucifer and Diana are shown here in very primitive guise. This hippogamous, if we may call it so, idea is not confined to Britain. Giraldus Cambrensis, when writing his twelfth-century account of Ireland, describes in shocked terms the induction of a king of Donegal. Although he does not more than hint at the actual mating, it is clear that the king had to behave as a stallion, going on all fours, and then, when the grey mare had been sacrificed, bathe in broth made from the carcass, drink it and eat the flesh. He was being turned into a stallion by magical rites."

The archaeologist Seton George discovered a succession of superimposed temples in Turkey which covered thousands of years of the Bronze Age, in which the symbolism of male and female fertility was presented with great simplicity and without change. Lethbridge says, "The horned altar to which the sacrifice was bound, as it says in the Bible, was found in the earliest temples right through to the latest. The Gods worshipped there were probably known as Baal and Ashtoreth."

J. A. MacCulloch, in his book *The Religion of the Ancient Celts,* mentions the altar of Cernunnos at Paris and describes other ancient religious artifacts depicting the Horned God:

> (a) A bronze statuette from Autun represents a similar figure, probably horned, who presents a torque to two ram's-headed serpents. Fixed above his ears are two small heads. On a monument from Vandoeuvres is a squatting horned god, pressing a sack. Two genii stand beside him on a serpent, while one of them holds a torque.
> (b) Another squatting horned figure with a torque occurs on an altar from Reims. He presses a bag, from which grain escapes, and on it an ox and stag are feeding. A rat is represented on the pediment above, and on either side stand Apollo and Mercury. On the altar at Saintes is a squatting

but headless god with torque and purse. Beside him is a goddess with a cornucopia, and a smaller divinity with a cornucopia and an apple. A similar squatting figure, supported by male and female deities, is represented on the other side of the altar. On the altar of Beaune are three figures, one horned with a cornucopia, another three-headed, holding a basket. Three figures, one female and two male, are found on the Dennevy altar. One god is three-faced, the other has a cornucopia which he offers to a serpent.

(c) Another image represents a three-faced God, holding a serpent with a ram's head.

(d) Above a seated god and goddess on an altar from Malmaison is a block carved to represent three faces. To be compared with these are seven steles from Reims, each with a triple face but only one pair of eyes. Above some of these is a ram's head. On eight stele the heads are separated.

MacCulloch points out that horned animals were used as symbols of the Deity and that Cernunnos was another form of the Celtic Dispater, though where one was found the other usually was not. They were all gods and goddesses of fertility and the underworld. He writes, "Cernunnos may thus have been regarded as a three-headed, horned, squatting god, with a torque and a ram's-headed serpent. But a horned god is sometimes a member of a triad, perhaps representing myths in which Cernunnos was associated with other gods. The three-headed god may be the same as the horned god, though on the Beaune altar they are distinct. The various representations are linked together, but it is not certain that all are varying types of one god. Horns, torque, horned snake, or even the triple head may have been symbols pertaining to more than one god, though generally associated with Cernunnos."

Ancient astrology and religious antiquity is indicated by the fact that nearly all the Old Religions had the bull (Taurus) as either an object of veneration or a sacrifice to the Gods. During the time when the sun rose in Taurus, nearly all the Sun Gods were portrayed wearing bull-horns on their heads. After the sun passed into the sign of Aries, many of the Gods were depicted wearing ram's heads. Indian tradition says that a major war broke out during the transition from Taurus to Aries, and for reasons known only to the priests, the ram was substituted for the previous bull as a sanctified symbol. This divided the people and bloody civil war was the result. Today modern Astrology gives Aries as the first sign and Taurus as the second one. Capricorn, the goat, another horned animal is the tenth sign of the zodiac. Ancient astro-religion associated the births and deaths of gods with the zodiacal signs and early Christian mystics attempted to harmonize the life of Jesus with this astrological tradition. Thus the Piscean Age has been dominated by Christianity. The Talmud calls the coming Messiah Dag, the fish, who was said to be reborn of the fish goddess Atergatis. Throughout the Christian story of Jesus, fishes play a prominent role: fishermen, "fishers of souls," the miracle of multiplying the loaves and fishes to feed the multitudes. Christians were called *pisiculi,* "little fishes," during the first four hundred years. Jesus himself was called the Big Fish. Amulets and icons depicted him in the form of a fish. This sign was also used on the catacombs and became the secret sign of Christians. In the second century Clement urged Christians to engrave a fish on their seals in order to distinguish them from the Pagans. Many mystics and psychics predict that the coming Age of Aquarius, the water bearer, spells an end to organized religion, especially Christianity, and that it will combine the best elements of a pagan past and modern thought culminating in the rise of various independent religious groups the world over. In the book *Predictions for 1973* by Glenn McWane, I made this prediction: "The rise of pagan religions worshipping the ancient gods and goddesses will see the establishment of public temples in many U.S. cities."

Witchcraft has gone back to its ancient roots: Reverence is paid to the Horned God and the Mother Goddess. The traditional coven of thirteen stems from the thirteen lunar cycles and is not a parody of Jesus and the twelve Apostles as some critics claim—in fact just the reverse. Many modern scholars believe that Jesus was an Essene; this sect was a secret society that had its roots in the worship of the Goddess Cybele, whose priests were eunuchs. It is believed that the thirty years of Jesus's life of which there is no record were spent as a eunuch priest devoted to Cybele.

St. Paul preached an Essene doctrine that showed complete contempt for the human body and urged that men and women abandon sex in marriage. In Matthew 19:12 it says, ". . . and there are some eunuchs, which were made eunuchs of men; and there be eunuchs, which have made themselves eunuchs for the kingdom of heaven's sake. He that is able to receive it, let him receive it." Celibacy is a modified form of this belief. Self-castration is the logical result for those who were fanatics in this faith. Such eunuch priests had no difficulty in preaching against something in which they could play no part. A deficiency was turned into a doctrine, self-mutilation into a new morality, a secret Essene practice into a Church ethic. Both sacrament and sacrifice come from the Latin word *sacer*, "sacred." But the Hebrew word *zakar* means "phallus." Of course the early Christians were Jews, and it is likely that when they came to Rome the two words became intermingled. It's also interesting to point out that the words *test, attest, testify,* and *testament* stem from the ancient practice of swearing an oath or taking a vow by placing one's hand on the testes of another. The sexual organs were considered sacred. The Bible is full of such references, most notably that of Solomon ascending the throne, when all the princes and notables attending at the time "gave their hand under Solomon" (I Chronicles 29:24f.).

There are numerous references to phallic worship in the Bible, but these have been disguised by Christian translators. The words "thigh" and "loins" are often euphemisms for phallus. In fact the word *bosheth,* a phallic pillar, is translated into "shame." Israelites made sacrifices to Baal-Peor. Baal was the God of generation; peor meant opening or womb; thus, worship of the male-female principle. In Genesis 32:30, it says Jacob wrestled with the Lord and saw his face, calling the place Peniel. El is a title given to God, and Peni is self-explanatory. The word "face" is another euphemism to describe the various aspects of a deity. When phallic worship was condemned, considered sacrilegious rather than sacred, it found expression in disguised forms. Horns, in one form or another, became unconscious substitutional phalli. Ask most men: What is the most sacred part of your body to you? From the answer it's not hard to see that would be his greatest sacrifice. Those who performed the "sacred sacrifice" would naturally want others to do the same. The have-nots resented the haves. Whether it was the horns of honor or just those who were plain horny, the technique was to instil guilt in those who retained their gonads. From Cybele to castration to celibacy, sex was turned into a hex, the natural became naughty, the sacred turned into the profane.

The worship of the Horned God has survived up to modern times in a disguised form. At Abbots Bromley, a village on the borders of Needwood Forest in Staffordshire, England, they had an annual celebration in which men wore deer skulls with antlers. They ran through the streets, singing and dancing, egged on by another man dressed as a horseman and carrying a whip. Another with a bow and arrow took make-believe potshots at the dancers, who represented deer. This Horn Dance was celebrated in September, the Sunday next to the fourth. The village vicar was in charge of keeping the hobbyhorse, the horns, the bow and arrow, and an old pot that was passed around to collect money. The horns were reindeer. The hobbyhorse was constructed of wood and cloth and its jaw worked by a string. It clacked to synchronize with the steps of the dancers. At one time this ceremony was performed during the Christmas season; the different dates stemmed from the many civil wars which interrupted the festivities from time to time. The money-pot was also a "loving cup" in which everyone took a sip of local ale.

Theodore, Archbishop of Canterbury (A.D. 668–690), in his *Liber Poenitentialis,* alluding to the ritual dances to the Horned God still flourishing after the advent of Christianity in England, said, "If anyone at the Kalends of January goes about as a stag or a bull; that is, making himself into a wild animal and dressing in the skin of a herd animal, and putting on the heads of beasts; those who in such wise transform themselves into the appearance of a wild animal, penance for three years because this is devilish."

Prohibitions or not, these dances continued. At the Puck Fair at Killorglin, Ireland, a billy-goat is crowned King Puck. Doreen Valiente in her *Where Witchcraft Lives* says, "Now, this gives us a clue as to who the original Puck of Pook's Hill was, here in Sussex. He was none other than the old god of the woods himself with all his traditional attributes. 'Puck' or 'Pouke' is Old English word for the Devil. Yet it forms part of many Sussex place-names, such as Pookhill, Puckscroft, Puckstye, Pookreed etc.

"Puck was also known as Robin Goodfellow. A woodcut illustrating an old chapbook called *The Mad Pranks of Robin Goodfellow*, dated 1628, shows him clearly in his character as the god of the witch-covens. Rough and crude as this old woodcut is, it is evident that it depicts a night dance of witches. The central figure is Puck himself, holding a broomstick in one hand and a lighted candle in the other. The coven, six men and six women placed alternately, dance around him in a ring, following a circle which is marked out upon the ground. Outside the circle are vessels holding food and drink, and a man playing music for the dancers. Owls flit through the night sky overhead. Seated outside the ring of dancers is an animal that looks like a witch's black cat."

Variations of the Horn Dance have occurred in many other countries, too. Up until the Communists took over Rumania after World War II, this was a national holiday celebrated on All Souls' Day. It has been traced to the Dionysian-Bacchic rites of antiquity, especially as practiced by the Maenads, all women. In his *Descriptio Moldaviae*, the Roumanian historian Cantemir describes the hobbyhorse dancers: "They dress like women; on their heads they put crowns of wormwood leaves and flowers. They speak in a thin, feminine voice and, in order not to be recognized, cover their faces with white veils." That was in the eighteenth century. Later the dancers up till recently represented the followers of Dionysius, the half-horse, half-men satyrs. Marcu Beza, in his *Paganism In Roumanian Folklore*, says, "Here we have the ancient god of fertility in a regular folk-play, which, containing all the elements of a Dionysian ritual, has survived down the centuries; for it has always possessed magical intention and been in keeping as well with the taste of the people. Both the dancing and the queer disguises have helped them to forget themselves, taken them away from everyday life and restrictions and brought them closer to nature, plunging them into rapturous joy, such as one might catch an echo of in the beautiful lines of Euripides:

And all the mountain felt
And worshipped with them, and the wild things knelt
And ramped and gloried, and the wilderness
Was filled with moving voices and dim stress."

In a footnote Mr. Beza says, "Since the above appeared in *Quest*, I came into touch with Percy Maylam's *Hooden Horse*, Canterbury, 1909. The description in it, as well as the photographs of hobby-horse forms used until very recently in East Kent, show a manifest similarity and identity of origin with the Roumanian custom."

The Puritan writer Stubbes, during the reign of Queen Elizabeth I, called the man, usually a poet or playwright responsible for the hobbyhorse pageants and known as the Lord of Misrule, "a grand captaine of mischiefe." The following is a summary of his minute description of the wild doings: After the Lord of Misrule is elected, he takes twenty to sixty others "lyke himself" to act as his guard, and they are decorated with ribbons, scarfs, and bells on their legs. They gather up their hobby-horses, dragons, horns, and drums and "strike up the devill's dance withal." They march to the church, invading it, even if in service, with so much noise that one can't hear his own voice. They go to the churchyard, set up booths; here drinking and dancing go on all day and night. They collect money and offer badges in return and don't hesitate to insult, and even duck, those who refuse to contribute.

Other remnants of these dances are the famous Mummers Parade held every year in Philadelphia, derived from the Roman Saturnalia. The word itself comes from the Dutch *Mumme* or *Momme,* a mask or disguise. The Welsh also had a custom of carrying a horse's skull at Christmas that was decorated with ribbons. This horse's head was called *Mari Lwyd,* which some have translated as "gray Mare." *Lywd* is gray, but *Mari* is not a mare in Welsh.

The horn and hobbyhorse dance are survivals of pagan fertility worship. Besides the hobbyhorse and other paraphernalia, there was also a man dressed as a woman and called Maid Marian. He carried a ladle, which, like the cup and caldron, is a symbol of femininity. The Fool is dressed like a court jester and carries a phallus. The interweaving of the six white-antlered dancers with the six blue-antlered dancers symbolizes sexual union for the purpose of fertility, a magic acting-out. Maid Marian is a surviving echo of the Great Mother Goddess, whose names were Mari, Mary, Marian, Miriam, Mariandyne, and Marriamne. *Ma-ri-enna* means "the fruitful mother of heaven." The name *Ma-ri* itself means "the fruitful mother," and *Ma* is a diminutive of the Sumerian *Ama* meaning "mother." Robert Graves in *The White Goddess* says that all of the above Mari-named goddesses are the ancient Sea-goddess Marian "in transparent disguise . . . patroness of poets and lovers and proud mother of the Archer of Love. Robin Hood in the ballads always swore by her. She was swarthy faced." He says that Robin Hood renamed his wife Matilda "Maid Marian," and judging from the early ballad *The Banished Man,* "must have cut her hair and put on male dress in order to belong to the outlaw fraternity, as in Albania to this day young women join male hunting parties, dress as men and are so treated—Atalanta and Calydon who took part in the hunt of the Calydonia Boar was the prototype. The outlaw band then formed a coven of thirteen with Marian acting as the *pucelle,* or maiden of the coven; presumably she wore her proper clothes in the May Day orgies as Robin's bride."

The name "Hood" itself meant "log," one cut from the sacred oak, and it was believed that it was this that Robin Hood rode to escape his enemies, called "Robin Hood's Steed." From this may have evolved the hobby-horse dance. As to the translation of the Welsh name for the horse's head, *Mari Lwyd,* from the above Mari is self-explanatory. *Lwyd* means gray or "swarthy-faced" as in Graves's description.

The Morris Dances took place on May Day with maypoles and a cast of characters featuring Robin

Hood, Little John, Friar Tuck, Maid Marian, and the hobbyhorse. And old ballad of 1614 says:

> It was my hap of late by chance
> To meet a country morris-dance,
> When, chiefest of them all, the foole
> Plaid with a ladle and a toole;
> When every younker shak't his hels
> And fine Maid Marian with her smoile,
> Showed how a rascal plaid the voile,
> And when the hobby-horse did wihy,
> Then all the wenches gave a tihy . . .

Christian chroniclers tried to attribute the name Morris Men to the *Moriscoes* or Morrish Men. But Robert Graves points out that the name Morris was originally written *maris,* which means that they were Mari's or Mary's men, sometimes called "morrice men" or Marian's merrymakers, or Robin Hood and his Merry Men. Today a common Witch greeting other than "Blessed Be" is "Merry meet . . . Merry Part."

Horns have always symbolized strength, courage, potency, and power. One of the earliest archaeological discoveries concerning man's use of horns was found in a middle paleolithic cave, Teshik-tash, in the Central Asian mountains of southwest Uzbekistan. In this Neanderthal burial site they discovered a boy ritually buried with his head surrounded by five pairs of ibex horns with their ends down in the earth. One can only try to imagine the reason for this. This has been dated as going back to 60,000 or 70,000 years ago. The cave of Les Trois Frères, featuring what has been called "The Horned Sorcerer," dates back 15,000 to 25,000 years. The "Venus of Laussel" is a rock carving of a Mother

Goddess holding a bison horn at Dordogne, dated back to the paleolithic period. Early man had to hunt for his food, and he came to respect the great herds of reindeer, bison, and other horned animals, especially their procreative abilities. The horns became talismans, magical amulets, symbols of both life and death. The Teutonic peoples identified with horned animals, and a figure of three interlocked horns was found on an ancient runestone in Snoldelev in Denmark. It is believed that this was a sign of the God Odin. The goat itself was a sign of the God Thor (or Donar). The Teutonic god Heimball was associated with the ram. The horned headdresses of the Scandinavians dating back to 2000 B.C. were worn by the Viking warriors up to A.D. 1000.

From the bull-gods of ancient India, Babylon, Egypt, and their incorporation into the Greco-Roman pantheon, down to modern-day Witchcraft, homage is paid to the Horned God. Many Old Religion rituals consist of the High Priestess placing a horned hat on the head of her High Priest. She herself wears a crescent-crown. The early Hebrews had a bull-god called the "Bull of Jacob." There was a clash between the bull-cult of Jacob and that of Moses. The ram too was sacred to the Jews, and its horn was called the *shofar*. It was used to represent the voice of God. The Minoan civilization of Crete was devoted to the bull-cult, and its King Minos was believed to be the incarnation of the Horned God, just as the High Priest in Witchcraft today is the direct representative of the Horned God. The high priestess is the direct representative of the Goddess on earth. Greek mythology calls Zeus the father of Greece; he was depicted with bull-horns, another god of fertility. His wife Hera was associated with the cow. At

Samos she is depicted on a wooden post with cow horns at the top. Pan and the Satyrs had goat horns. Ionic architecture is a modified form of horn symbolism. Italy, Sardinia, Sicily—in fact nearly all of the Mediterranean islands—have uncovered images of the Horned God. Etruscan art shows a river god with horns. Mithras, the rival religion of early Christianity, was associated with the bull-cult and considered the Lord of Fecundity. Persian, Hindu, and Buddhist religions had both gods and demons that were horned. In the Council of Toledo (447), the Devil was defined as "a large, black monstrous apparition with horns on his head, cloven hoofs . . . an immense phallus, and a sulphurous smell."

The root word *div* or *dev* can apply to both divinities or devils. In the chapter on the Yezidis in my *Black Magic, Satanism, and Voodoo,* I wrote, "Whether demon or divine all depends on who's doing the calling. All the gods of ancient Greece and Rome were considered devils by the early Christians. The goat-god of the Witches became the Christian devil. Islamism degraded all the pagan gods into jinn. In every world religion the other person's gods were demons or devils. . . . theirs was the 'only true God.' The word *deva* is applied to the gods of India while this same word means demons (devils in Persia (Iran). Another juxtaposition is that the word *asura* is the name of the friendly gods of Persia while in India it is applied to demons. . . . In the remote past it's possible that the ancestors of both Hindus and Persians were united in their beliefs until a religious schism took place. A cuneiform text, discovered at Pterium, in the center of Asia Minor, says that about fourteen hundred years before Christ, certain tribes had as their gods Mithra, Indra,

Varuna and Nasatyas. The first two are well known in both India and Persia, while the latter two are native to India."

Celtic Horned Gods were usually depicted with stag antlers, most notable that of Cernunnos. In the ancient sanctuary of Val Canonica, in northern Italy, he is carved on a rock with antlers and wearing a torque (neck ornament). This is dated at the fourth century B.C. There is a famous silver bowl found at Jutland, in a bog at Gundestrup. His head is adorned with exaggerated antlers. A deer is to his right with the same antlers. On his left is a wolf. There are other animals. The antlered deity sits in mastery over all. In Lady Charlotte Guest's translation of *The Mabinogion* is the story of "The Lady Of The Fountain," in which is prophesied that Cynon, son of Clydno, will meet a huge black man twice his size, one-footed and one-eyed, sitting in the middle of the forest, surrounded by wild animals gazing at him. The prophecy is fulfilled, and Cynon asks the man, "What is your power over animals?" He grabs his club, strikes a stag who gives out a loud cry, and all the wild animals of the forest flock to him, bowing their heads "even as humble subjects would do to their lord."

The Celts also had ram-headed Horned Gods, as well as those depicting the bull horns, often associated with Mercury. These were usually war or fertility gods. Early Welsh triads have many references to "bull warriors." Irish mythology has the great bull the Donn of Cualnge. His rival was the Findbennach, the "White Horned." He was a warrior god of the pastoral, warlike society, protector and provider, and the maker of magical music. Christianity robbed the Celts of their pagan, primitive, deeply rooted, unconsciously remembered, emotionally felt past whose stirrings have finally broken through the surface. Many feel the call and are now rediscovering a part of themselves so long lost by participating in the religions of their ancestors. Proudly pagan, the Way of the Wicca is constantly being given new impetus as the following story in the October 30, 1972, *Time* magazine illustrates.

In the science section of *Time* magazine there appeared an article entitled "The Valley of Marvels." This was located in the high Alps of southeastern France. The only people who ever got to it were mountain climbers and shepherds. It was six thousand feet from the village of St. Dalmas-de-Tende, thirty miles northeast of Nice. Those who did brought back tales of mysterious rock carvings. No one could explain them until a French archaeologist made an on-site study.

"Henry de Lumley," *Time* says, "who has led many teams of volunteer explorers into the valley during snow-free summer months, believes that the primitive art was inscribed between 1800 B.C. and 1500 B.C. Thus the carvings belong 'not to prehistory but to protohistory—that period of roughly 2000 years between prehistoric times and recorded history.' De Lumley's dating involved shrewd detective work in museums. The short, triangular dagger blades portrayed in many of the engravings, for instance, closely resemble artifacts already identified as products of early Bronze Age (1800 B.C.–1500 B.C.) civilizations in the Rhone Valley and Swiss Lake villages. Other daggers with either oval or elongated blades, concave edges and T-shaped hilts are typical of middle Bronze Age weapons made between 1500 B.C. and 1100 B.C."

The next two paragraphs are of immense interest

to students of ancient religions, modern Pagans, and especially Witches:

> The engravings include a rich but baffling array of symbols. The most frequently recurring images are horned figures—what de Lumley calls "stylized cattle." There are also daggers, crosslike inscriptions, stars and geometric forms, all of which may have had religious significance. Only a few hundred of the 37,000 engravings catalogued thus far portray human figures: one example, known as the "Chief Of The Tribe," *shows a man formed almost entirely out of horn symbols.*
>
> With the aid of a computer at the University of Aix-Marseille, De Lumley hopes eventually to index all of the valley's more than 200,000 engravings. That could help him to interpret the obscure symbols and learn more about the men who carved them. All that he will say now is that the valley *"appears to have been a sacred place in the Bronze Age.* But by the beginning of the first millenium (100 B.C.) its message was lost." [Italics added]

De Lumley had better work fast or get Government protection, because the article states that a horde of tourists and souvenir collectors use chalk and stone on the engravings in order to get better photographs. Some vandals have even carted off entire slabs. De Lumley said, "If this keeps up, in 50 years the Valley of Marvels, the most remarkable cultural treasure of the Alps, will have been destroyed."

5

Sicilian Witchcraft

There are over 250 different dialects in Italy. Northerners seldom understand Southerners, and vice versa. Many Italians don't consider the Sicilians as one of themselves, and the latter are fiercely proud of being Sicilian. Geologists have proven via deep-sea soundings that Sicily and Tunisia were connected by a land mass centuries ago. They discovered many bones of extinct tropical animals who wandered by land from Africa to southern Europe. Then there was a sinking of the land mass, and the waters of the Atlantic rushed in through the opening now known as the Straits of Gibraltar, connecting the Atlantic with the Mediterranean.

In the ninth century before Christ, or about one hundred years before Rome was founded, the Tyrian Colony of Carthage, which reigned as a gloriously rich country for seven hundred years, master of the sea, flourished directly opposite the largest Mediterranean island of Sicily. The latter at the time was called Trinacria and was literally the center of the civilized world. It was both equidistant from Spain and Egypt (East and West) and equidistant from Rome and Carthage (North and South). Only a two-mile strait separated it from Italy, of which it was once a part. Its triangular shape gave it the name of Trinacria. Till this day Sicily's symbol is the head with three legs. In ancient times the symbol contained the head of Medusa with three legs, like a jewel with three facets turned towards Europe, Asia, and Africa.

For three thousand years, because of its geographical desirability and natural beauty, Sicily was ravaged by Phoenicians, Greeks, Romans, Carthaginians, Arabs, Goths, Byzantines, Normans, French, Spaniards, and Italians. All of them contributed to its culture, left their impact, which the Sicilians absorbed. Its history is so interwoven with that of Greece and Rome that Goethe once said, "Italy without Sicily leaves no image in the soul; Sicily is the key to all."

Called "the garden of the Mediterranean" because of its fertile wheat-producing fields—also the "Granary of Rome"—legend tells us that it was the favorite home of the Goddess of agriculture, called Demeter by the Greeks and Ceres by the Romans. It was near Lake Pergusa, situated in the center of Sicily, that her daughter Persephone (Greek) or Proserpina (Roman) was abducted into the underworld by Pluto while she was gathering flowers. Some lines depicting the mourning of the Earth Mother Goddess Demeter for her lost Persephone were quoted by John L. Stoddard in his book, *Lectures:*

> What ails her that she comes not home?
> Demeter seeks her far and wide,
> And, gloomy-browed, doth ceaseless roam
> From many a morn till eventide.
> 'My life, immortal though it be,
> Is naught,' she cries, 'for want of thee,
> Persephone! Persephone!

Demeter lit a torch at Mount Etna to help her in her search. She wandered frantically over many lands, finally returning to Sicily in despair. She learned from the river nymph Cyane of what happened to her kidnapped daughter. She threatened the earth with famine, unless Persephone was restored to her. Jove promised her that Persephone would be returned to her at the spring of each year. The other half of the year she would have to reside with Pluto. In those times the seasons were divided into two: summer and winter. Spring began around April or May and ended by harvest time, in the autumn.

John L. Stoddard, in his "Lectures," says, "Perhaps, like most of the legends of antiquity, this fable was purely allegorical, and parabled the fact that seed, when planted in the ground, lies hidden in the earth, until in spring it rises from the darkness of the underworld into the light of day. At all events, it is undoubtedly true that every year, for centuries, when verdure once more crept mysteriously over the Sicilian fields, and all the mountain sides grew radiant with vernal bloom, the people reveled in the restoration of Persephone; and in the autumn also, when the golden grain had all been garnered, they celebrated joyfully the festival of Ceres (Demeter), decking their hair with ears of wheat and corn-flowers, just as the happy Goddess had adorned her own fair tresses in the joy of being reunited with her child."

Even today there are obvious remnants of the worship of Demeter and Persephone. During the feasts of the Catholic Madonna (patterned upon Demeter, though this may be unknown to the worshippers), devout Catholics place before her statue gifts of flowers and sheaves of grain, while white-robed worshippers walk from shrine to shrine holding flower-garlands in their hands. They sprinkle their fields with holy water at the time of planting and take their seeds to be blessed by the church. During harvest time they bring to the church their first cereals in thanks to the favors of Demeter (Ceres), now transformed into the Madonna.

Sicily abounds with the ruins of ancient temples, now only pitiful reminders of their former grandeur. Most of them were built upon hilltops and mountains. Besides those dedicated to Demeter and Persephone there are numerous relics from the temples dedicated to such ancient Gods and Goddesses as Venus, Neptune, Juno, Vulcan, Diana, Hercules, Enceladus, Pluto, Minerva, and many others. The famous Temple to Demeter in Enna (now called Castrogiovanni and listed as such on tourist maps, underground *strege* although always call it by its former name, Enna) was built upon the very site of another ancient Goddess of the Sikels, who had the same attributes as the Greek Goddess. Her secret name, which has been preserved for centuries, is known only to those who have been initiated into her worship. She was supplanted by the Greek Demeter, who in turn was supplanted by the Christian Madonna.

To quote from the *WICA Newsletter:* "Sad to see Persephone's famous Lake Pergusa now overrun with water weeds. The water is brackish. At one far end is a small grove of eucalyptus trees. Surrounding the lake is an auto race track. Enna is high on a hill overlooking the lake, a valley, and in one of the low cliffs there is a dark cave which the local inhabitants will tell you is the one through which Pluto abducted Persephone into the underworld. Enna is one of Sicily's highest cities. On top of the remains of a citadel was situated the world-famous Temple of Demeter. The rock itself is shaped somewhat like a ship. In the east one can face the snowy cone of Mount Etna. Here too is the famous Madonna with a *female* Jesus, unknown to most of the locals and never seen by tourists. The small church in which it resides is hidden by a courtyard in which various peasants sell their wares. I'm deeply indebted to my strege relatives who took me to see it in 1964."

The sculptor who made the Madonna with a female Jesus belonged to *la vecchia religione*—the Old Religion—and in this way paid tribute to his Goddesses, Demeter and Persephone. Shrewdly he realized that no one would look too closely under the "swaddling clothes" to determine if their "Jesus" was male or female. Even the thought would have been considered sacrilegious. He counted on their taking for granted that the Madonna's child was a male Jesus. Old Religionists knew better and had many a laugh over it.

I visited Sicily in 1964 while living in Tangier, Morocco and I met many of my *strege* relatives for the first time. In spite of the fact that I don't speak Italian fluently, or the Sicilian dialect for that matter, we managed to communicate completely with much goodwill, joy and laughter (especially when I thought I was saying one thing and my pronunciation made it something else to the delight of my relatives and other strege friends!).

That same *WICA Newsletter* gave a brief description of other Sicilian temples. Here are some of them: "SEGESTE: All that remains today of Segeste's Temple of Demeter are 36 massive columns without a roof. Goethe wrote about it: "A shrill wind whistled through the columns as if through a wood, and screaming birds of prey hovered around the pediments." Agathocles of Syracuse conquered Segeste and in the year 900 it was totally destroyed. The Temple of Demeter that was under construction was never completed."

'SYRACUSE faces the sea. It has the 'ear of Dionysius' a cave 75 feet high and 200 feet deep. Guides will tell you 'The cave's acoustical properties amplify every sound a hundred times. Dionysius used it to eavesdrop on the conversations of prisoners below.' The Temple of Minerva is now the Cathedral of Syracuse, a place of worship for twenty five centuries. In ancient times sailors could see the statue of the Goddess far out at sea. It was saved from destruction in the 7th Century by a Bishop who converted it into a Catholic Church. Then the Saracens turned it into a Mosque. The Normans once again made it Christian. The earthquake of 1693 destroyed the Norman facade. It has since been rebuilt.

TAORMINA is built on the ancient city of Naxos, which was destroyed by Dionysius. In 1953 fishermen discovered an ancient temple there at the bottom of the sea. They found a rich vein of archaeological artifacts, coins and vases. Taormina-itself is one of Sicily's most beautiful cities.

TYNDARI: This is the home of the mysterious and famous "Black Madonna." She is jet black, her African origin obvious. Her child is also black. They wear gold jewel-encrusted crowns, jewelled robes made of ivory and gold. There are many legends surrounding her. One is that she was either a black princess or a statue which was thrown from a ship into the sea. She walked ashore to Tyndari and the violent storm ceased. The Byzantine ships sailed for home.

Sicilian tradition, like other countries, peoples its land with Gods and Goddesses, both benevolent and malevolent, and then giants which Homer refers to in his *Odyssey:* Cyclops, Lotophagi, and Laistrygones. These were followed by the Sikans, the Sikels, the Sircanians, and Elymians. The Sikels were blood-brothers to the pioneers of Rome and Tuscany. Legend says they settled in Sicily about 1100 B.C. and gave the island its present name. Homer's *Odyssey* tells us that Penelope's suitors threatened to sell the disguised Odysseus to the Sikels as a slave. Even old Laertes had a Sikelian slave woman. The wily Phoenicians, called Canaanites in the Old Testament, told such stories to frighten away other explorers. Though they spoke Hebrew, they worshipped Baal and Ashtoroth, the services often consisting of human sacrifice. Probably their greatest contribution to all of Europe was the alphabet. Their rivals, the Greeks brought their own culture to Sicily and considered it a western colony. Trinakria, the Three Promontories, became a second Greek world, and Syracuse rivaled Athens in culture, wisdom, and beauty. It was founded in 734 B.C. by Dorian Greeks from Corinth.

A partial list of the immortals of literature who either visited Sicily or made it their permanent home include Pindar, a poet whose lyrics record much of early Sicilian history; the poetess Sappho, equally renowned for her beautiful poetry and Lesbian loves; Aeschylus, poet and playwright; Epicharmus, originator of a certain type of Sicilian comedy; Empedocles of

Akragas, most distinguished of Sicilian philosophers, poets, and physicians; Philistus and Diodoros of Agyrium, major historians; Archimedes, world-famous mathematician; Theocritus, who gave the world its first pastorals and bucolics, hauntingly sweet music that even today shepherds play to their flocks, unaware of their origins centuries ago.

The Phoenicians, the Greeks, the Saracens, and all the other conquerors kept Sicily in a constant state of turmoil and warfare. But they all left their traces. They all contributed to its culture. The very Italian language itself was developed in the court of Emperor Frederick II at Palermo. He was both emperor of Germany and king of Sicily, and a constant thorn in the side of the Popes. After his death the Pope gave the Crown of Sicily to Count Charles of Anjou, who let his lieutenants rule the country as they wished. Sixteen years later, in 1282, they paid dearly for their misrule. All the Sicilians rose up as one and slaughtered every man, woman, and child connected with their oppressors. This is known in history as the Sicilian Vespers. They requested that Don Pedro of Aragon, son of Manfred, their last Norman king, to rule them. This lasted till 1409. Then the country was governed by indifferent Spanish viceroys up till the beginning of the eighteenth century. From her former glory Sicily was now merely a grubby appendage and pawn in the power-plays of other nations. Finally Giuseppe Garibaldi with his immortal "thousand" freed all of Sicily and Italy from the foreign oppressors.

Arthur Stanley Riggs, in his *Vistas In Sicily* says, "So it is clear that there has never been a Sicilian nation, nor has there ever been a Sicilian language; but every great race that dwells about the Mediterranean at some time has had a part in Sicily's story, and each race in its turn has left an indelible imprint upon language and customs, upon architecture and people. Here one sees a pure Greek face of classic beauty; there a Saracen gazes calmly upon us out of features which could come only from the burning desert and the infinite starry night in the open; and, yonder, a Roman, proud and silent, bends to toil the Romans of old never knew. On many a hill rises the matchless, mellow ruin of a Greek temple, lovely as anything Greece itself can show; and in the cities the architectonic genius and spirit of the races blend in structures dignified and massive, or light and airy almost to the point of being fantastic."

No, this is not a history book about Sicily. The above brief sketch is necessary to show the myriad threads that go into making the Sicilian *strega* tapestry. I think the best concrete illustration of this is the aforementioned Cathedral of Syracuse, described as "a queer combination of battlemented Moorish castle, ancient Greek temple and modern Christian structure." First it was a Temple to Minerva built in the sixth century B.C., then a Christian Church under the direction of Bishop Zosimus of Syracuse. The Saracens turned it into a mosque in A.D. 878. For two centuries the muezzins chanted the praises of Allah and Muhammad from its historic walls. Then the Normans came. Once again it became Christian. The earthquake of 1693 destroyed part of it. It was rebuilt and now is the diocesan church of Syracuse. Though there still is archaeological dispute as to which ancient deity was worshipped there, some ascribing it to Minerva, others to Diana, the street arabs will tell you in no uncertain terms that it's the *tempio di Diana*.

Sicilian Witchcraft

Cicero's description of the Temple of Minerva (Athena) seems to place that one in a different location. He says, ". . . a great brazen shield overlaid with gold, which served as a landmark to sailors on entering the port. The folding doors of ivory and gold were also adorned with a marvelous golden head of Medusa." All these treasures were stolen. The prejudice of male chauvinist archaeologists is evident in their constantly attributing ancient temple ruins to male rather than female deities. One example is the ruins of the temple of Diana, Goddess of the hunt, not far away, which they now attribute to Apollo.

With all of these different cultures invading Sicily, the people had a wide variety of religious beliefs from which to choose. And even when the dominant religion was enforced, it was very difficult to get people to change their deep-rooted beliefs. Sicilians became adept in the art of survival, adopting whatever religious pose was most expedient. Always pragmatists, their attitude towards the various Gods and Goddesses was, "If you don't shape up you can be replaced." This was illustrated a few years ago when a visitor from Rome saw a Sicilian peasant woman shaking her fist at the Madonna and even spitting into the statue's face! The Catholic visitor was shocked. The local and wise priest told him, "Don't alarm yourself. She has reason. She's been praying for over three months, lighting candles, and her prayers haven't been answered." A Sicilian friend of mine, told me that his grandmother would turn the statue of the Madonna on its head when her prayers weren't answered. Even today some of them will lock up various saints in a dark closet if they don't come through.

In the March, 1972, *Occult Trade Journal*, Tom

Merlin discussed some comments of mine in a previous issue:

> In your December issue . . . I understand an observation was made that *Aradia* was used as the basis for the Gardnerian branch of Witchcraft. An examination of the portions of Gardnerian materials which have been published (in the books dealing with Alexander Sanders and the earlier works by Gerald Gardner) rather clearly shows the Gardnerian Craft to be primarily Celtic and British in its origins. It is particularly revealing to compare modern works on Gardnerian Witchcraft with earlier studies of Celtic supernatural traditions, such as those done by Fiona Macleod at about the turn of the century.
>
> *Aradia,* on the other hand, is quite purely a work dealing with Italian Witchcraft. Doubtless a few odds and ends have been borrowed by witches of other traditions; this borrowing is the rule rather than the exception in the witch cult. But certainly no British or Celtic witch would use a spell or incantation which crudely threatens the Deities! Yet this is done in *Aradia,* and quite often.
>
> The book may have its faults, due perhaps to the somewhat decadent state of the Italian Witchcraft at the time it was compiled. It is not, by any means, the basis of Gardnerian witchcraft. But it is well worth reading, and owning.*

---

* Margaret Murray's preface to her *Witch Cult In Western Europe* says, "It is more difficult to trace the English practices than the Scotch or French, for in England the cult was already in a decadent condition when records were made."

My reply to the above was, "If the state of Italian Witchcraft was decadent the British variety was practically nonexistent." But the above letter is true in one important respect: Unlike most other Witchcraft traditions, the Sicilian and some of the Italian branches do not hesitate to threaten the deities. They are not restricted by the Judeo-Christian-Moslem "one God" concept. And though British varieties do say that "The Gods need our help as much as we need theirs," the above letter indicates that in a showdown they don't demonstrate this belief. This Sicilian quality is not one of disrespect or blasphemy. It is one of positive self-assertion, a recognition of our own inner divinity, and a sense of personal power in our own lives that neither man nor God nor Goddess can undermine. Pragmatically it's Karmic: "as ye sow so shall ye reap," tit for tat, we respect you, you respect us. Since we identify with our Goddess so closely, and her Horned God consort, there is no sense of being inferior (which in itself would be a denial of such identification). And if no British or Celtic Witch would "crudely threaten the deities," the Sicilian *strege* have no dread of their version of Andred, they don't pander to Pan, and don't kowtow to Karnayna!

Centuries ago Old Religionists formed guerrilla bands in the mountains of Sicily. They fought both an oppressive Church and State. Secret societies were formed, Brotherhoods of Believers, Sisterhoods of Strege, militant-mystic *magi* who were determined to keep to the old ways, to resist all conquerors, who followed the adage "The best way to beat an enemy is to join him." This they did by raising some of their children in the Old Faith secretly, although publicly they were brought up to be Catholic priests. In times of danger they went to these *strege* priests. During Holy Communion the priest would warn his secret brethren of danger by slightly bending the host before placing it on the communicant's tongue. Publicly these *strege* priests were the most fanatic in their Catholic faith, above suspicion, dedicated to Christian dogma. Many people were burned in the Inquisitional insanity, but very few *strege* were caught. Those few were the result of accident, the accusations of spiteful or jealous neighbors, "Witchcraft" used then in the same way that "Communist" was used during the McCarthy period. Nor was it difficult for members of the underground faith to pray and light candles to the Madonna and Child, since they knew that she was merely another representation of their Goddess, whether called Diana, Minerva, Athene, Demeter, Persephone, Ashtoroth, or the secret Sikelian name.

It is believed that the early Sikels sailed on rafts from mainland Italy to Sicily and that they were part of the same stock that made up the Etruscans. This is why the book *Aradia* is so fascinating in many places. And T. C. Lethbridge's comments that it is somewhat marred by political propaganda can only be understood in the light of the above historic facts. This propaganda, though, is not derived from Middle Ages controversies, as it is from a history of over three thousand years of oppression. I cover our own traditions briefly in my book *Curses In Verses* in the somewhat misnamed "Roman Robin Hoods":

> ROMAN ROBIN HOODS
> In Old Sicily
> Oppressive cruelty
> Practised by the few
> Lordly rich who slew
> The peasants galore

Sicilian Witchcraft

But they kept their lore
Fleeing to the hills
Tending their wine stills
And hiding in caves
From those who made slaves
A guerilla band
In Sicilian land
Against Church and State
Nourished by their hate
Of oppressive laws
Slave-fought "Holy Wars"
Roman Robin Hoods
Fighting from the woods
Old Religion kept
While oppressors slept
Their Goddess adored
While Mafia lured
Hated enemy
O! so craftily
With Diana's aid
Kings' men waylaid
Queen of the Witches:
"Kill the sons of bitches!
Who murdered your wives
Took your babies' lives
Made your lives a hell
By sound of Church bell
Priest and prince have lied
While your loved ones died
Send them to their graves
Those who made you slaves
Keep the sacred rites
On moon-filled Sabbat nights
My daughter who came

Aradia by name
To help make you strong
Teaching right from wrong
With arrow and bow
Fight the evil foe
With water and wine
And salt while you dine
Blessed Sabbat keep
And the harvest reap
Eat Horned honey cakes
And fish from the lakes
Forest full of plants
Sing healing herb chants
While dressing your wounds
Fight the Papal goons
Form an underground
Where you can't be found
To the Craft be true
It will protect you
Should you in this fail
Your fate is the jail
Or even much worse
Is your self-made curse
Mafia became
In time a Craft shame
Roman Robin Hoods
Now just stolen goods
Robbing rich and poor
Just another whore
A few broke away
Faith held to this day
An underground spring
The Sicilians sing
And from their ovens

Sicilian Witchcraft

These secret covens
Continue to bake
Their salted Craft cake
Traditionalists
Old Religionists
Keeping the Craft true
And with it they grew
The sign of the Cross
For the Christian boss
And public prayer
But 'neath the layer
Benevento played
Wreaths for Goddess laid
Under church's nose
Planted a Craft rose
And the rosary
Fingered sorcery
Ave Maria
Ave Diana
Achieving their ends
With their Maltese friends
Ships with Eye of Horus
Craft singing chorus
How Old Religion
Was not clay pigeon
Pretending to be
Part of Holy See
And some became priests
Keeping Sabbat feasts
Thus able to spy
On the Christian lie
And of danger warn
Before deadly dawn
Written on Wafer

Mass was much safer
Holy Communion
A Craft reunion
Thus few Witches burned
Papal secrets learned
Diana's sentries
In Christian countries
Sounded the alarm
Preventing Witch harm
Only a few lost
In this holocaust
Strege are now strong
Still fighting the wrong
Robin Hoods today
For whom people pray
Still serving their needs
By word and Craft deeds.

The reference to Mafia above requires clarification. Sicily, because of its constant conquest by other nations, became a country of secret societies. And for every new organization there was a parent one no longer in existence. Sicilians were by nature antiestablishment and in self-protection banded together in various organizations. Since they could not achieve justice by the indifferent foreign rulers, who kept changing, each new conqueror bringing in a whole new set of harsh laws and religious ideas, secret societies with oaths of initiation, blood vows, and code words were inaugurated. Centuries ago these were made up mainly of the Old Religionists. They were literally the Italo-Sicilian version of Robin Hood and his "Merry Men," except that these men were in dead earnest. Their joy was given full reign only when they worshipped in the woods on moon-filled nights while armed sentries guarded all passes to their mountain retreats. At first defenders of the faith, the poor, and the oppressed, some of them became power-mad and worked for the feudal lords. They gradually dropped the worship of the Goddess and became an all-male-chauvinist society. They retained some of the rituals for initiation purposes but dropped, and eventually lost, both the worship and the origins of their rites. There were many schisms, splits, offshoots, and formations of rival societies.

Researchers to date have only been able to trace the origin of the word *Mafia* to one Mazzini in 1859. He only trusted those people who made up the underworld of society: thieves, prostitutes, and the like. He first called his society the *Oblinica,* coined from the Latin words *obelus,* "a spit," and *nico,* "I beckon." It meant "I beckon with a spit." "Spit" here is the name of an iron rod pointed at the end, really a dagger, so it means "I beckon with my knife." From this Mazzini formed an inner-sanctum society with blood oaths and initiation ceremonies. They were called the *Mafiosi,* which came from *Mafia,* which in turn is alleged to have been made up of the initials of the following five words: *Mazzini, autorizza, furti, incendi, avvelenamenti.* Translated, it means Mazzini authorizes thefts, arson, and poisoning. They called their crimes *pavi,* "bread," since it was by them that they lived.

Prior to the emergence of the Mafia as a criminal society, it was preceded by many others, such as the *Mala Vita*—"evil life"—which was taken from a novel by Degio Como, published before 1891. The *Camorra* was headquartered in Naples, and the word comes from the Spanish. It means a quarrel or dispute. The word

Camorrista means a quarrelsome person. The society's origins are traced to 1820. One of the most powerful societies were the *Carbonari,* literally the "charcoal burners." Some of its offshoots were the *Guelphic Knights,* the *Latini,* and the *Centres.* Most of them forbade anything to be written down, and many consisted of cells as small as two, to prevent discovery and betrayal. One of the most dangerous and powerful criminal groups was the *Decisi*—"the decided—"headed by Ciro Annichiarico, a renegade Catholic priest who committed murder and believed himself immortal. It took twenty-two bullets to finally kill him, and only the last one did it. One of the soldiers said, "As soon as we perceived that he was enchanted, we loaded his own musket with a silver ball, and this destroyed the spell."

Another society with mystic overtones was the *Calderari* which was thought to originate in Naples but really began in Palermo. They were tradesmen dealing in braziers (*calderari,* "caldrons"). Before that they were called the *Trinitarii* and were involved in insurrection against the French government. Both the Independents and the Delphic Priesthood worked for the unification of Italy and Sicily as one country; their goal, to once and for all throw off the yoke of foreign rule. The latter society's Delphic Priests said, "My mother has the sea for her mantle, high mountains for her scepter." When asked, "Who's your mother?" they replied, "The lady with the dark tresses, whose gifts are beauty, wisdom, and formerly strength: whose dowry is a flourishing garden, full of fragrant flowers, where bloom the olive and the vine; and who now groans, stabbed to the heart."

What is of interest here is that the code of honor called the omertà by the Mafia, with its accompaniment of vendetta, where any wrong done in this life must be avenged in this life, is the living out of the Law of Karma—"As ye sow so shall ye reap"—a tenet of all Witches, except that true Old Religionists do *not* take the law into their own hands. But like everyone else, they do have the moral right to self-defense, and it is applied according to the circumstances. Many of the Mafia initiation rituals were not invented by Mazzini, but were incorporated by him. Their origins lie in antiquity and are now perverted rites that were once sacred to *la vecchia religione*. The kiss, the blood oath, the vow never to reveal the secrets, the use of the knife, even the word *Mafia* itself, have an entirely different, but no longer used, meaning to the Sicilian *strege* who make up one branch of the many traditions in that multidimensional country. I can give one clue: The word itself is an anagram which means "faithful adoration of the Mother." It stems from the Latin words *mater*, meaning "mother," and *fidelitas*, "faithfulness." The "Mother" here is not the Christian Madonna but the ancient Earth Mother Goddess Demeter.

Another theory amongst *strege* is that it stems from the old Latin word of *filialis*, from *filius*, "son," and *filia*, "daughter." This also makes sense, since the Christian Madonna and child (male) has its precedent in the Goddess Demeter (Mater, Mother, "Ma") and her daughter Persephone (*filia*). The colloquial expression "Ma" for mother is also the name of another Goddess. Thus, *Mater filia* (mother-daughter) abbreviated into the code word, *Mafia*. It's my opinion that Mazzini corrupted the word for his own purposes, and attributed each of its letters to represent his own criminal intentions. What in the dim distant past began as an idealistic organization to fight wrongs, to achieve justice, to "rob the rich and give to the poor," degenerated into robbing as a way of life. Those who first began to fight for the oppressed in time joined the oppressors and became themselves oppressors. There was no more faith—just force. The devout secret *strege* stayed completely underground.

My own ancestry ranges from the Italians in northern Italy where there is a town of Martello, in the valley of Martello, down to Milan, where Aldo Martello was a famous platemaker and publisher reproducing the art of Leonardo da Vinci and Michelangelo, to Sicily where the maternal grandparents of Count Allessando Cagliostro (né Giuseppe Balsamo) were Matteo and Maria Martello, and where the Simeto is one of its principal rivers, having as one of its tributaries another called the Martello. The Martello coat of arms features a hammer with three stars above it. *Martello* means "hammer." However, the true symbol is a combination hammer on one side and ax on the other, a two-in-one implement similar to the labrys, or double-headed ax. There is more Sicilian in me now than there is Italian, and this takes me to my own *strege* heritage and once again to the town of Castrogiovanni, the Ancient Enna.

This is an ancient Sikel or Sikan town, 3,270 feet above sea level, one of the highest in Sicily. It is prehistoric and was seized by the Syracusans in 403 B.C. It was captured by the Carthaginians in the First Punic War, 258 B.C. Then through treachery the Romans conquered it. In 134 B.C. Enna became famous for its First Slave War when the inhabitants revolted. In A.D. 859 it was captured by the Saracens. In 1080 the Normans took it. The name Castrogiovanni is a corruption of the Saracen Casr-Janni, the fortress at Enna, one of the strongest natural fortresses in the world before modern artillery. Here is the once holy Lake Pergusa dominated by Mount Etna, and the site of the Temple to Demeter (or Ceres) across a ravine from Manfred's castle. Two of its columns are preserved in the small church of Saint Biagio. The Prospetto of the sacristy is formed of the antique apophyge, well preserved, and the Tribunal in which Cicero collected the charges against Verres and promised the Sicilians, especially the men of Enna, to help them. In Cicero's *Verres*, translated by Bohn, he says:

> It is an old opinion, O Judges, which can be proved from the most ancient records and monuments of the Greeks, that the whole island of Sicily was consecrated to Ceres and Libera. Not only did all the other nations think so, but the Sicilians themselves were so convinced of it that it appeared a deeply rooted and innate belief in their minds. For they believe that these goddesses were born in these districts, and that corn was first discovered in this land, and that Libera was carted off, the same goddess whom they call Proserpina, from a grove in the territory of Enna, a place which, because it is situated in the centre of the island, is called the navel of Sicily. And when Ceres wished to see her and trace her out, she is said to have lit her torches at those flames which burst out at the summit of Etna, and carrying these torches before her, to have wandered over the whole earth. But Enna, where those things I am speaking of are said to have been done, is in a high and lofty situation, on the top of which is a large level plain and springs of water which are never dry.

And the whole of the plain is cut off and separated, so as to be difficult of approach. Around it are many lakes and groves, and beautiful flowers at every season of the year, so that the place itself seems to testify to that abduction of the virgin which we have heard of from our boyhood. Near it is a cave turned towards the north, of unfathomable depth, where they say that Father Pluto suddenly rose out of the earth in his chariot and carried off the virgin from that spot, and that on a sudden, at no great distance from Syracuse, he went down beneath the earth, and that immediately a lake sprang up in that place; and there to this day the Syracusans celebrate anniversary festivals with a most numerous assemblage of both sexes. . . .

"For thoughts of that temple, of that place, of that holy religion come into my mind. Everything seemed present before my eyes, the day on which, when I arrived at Enna, the priests of Ceres came to meet me with garlands of vervain and with fillets; the concourse of citizens, among whom, while I was addressing them, there was much weeping and groaning that the most bitter grief seemed to have taken possession of the whole. They did not complain of the absolute way in which the tenths were levied, nor of the plunder of property, nor of the iniquity of tribunals, nor of that man's unhallowed lusts, nor of his violence, nor of the insults by which they had been oppressed and overwhelmed. It was the divinity of Ceres, the antiquity of their sacred observances, the holy veneration due to their temple, which they wished should have atonement made to them by the punishment of that most audacious and atrocious man. They said that they could endure anything else; that to everything else they were indifferent. This indignation of theirs was so great that you might suppose that Verres, like another king of hell, had come to Enna, and had carried off, not Proserpina, but Ceres herself. And, in truth, that city does not appear to be a city, but a shrine of Ceres. The people of Enna think that Ceres dwells among them, so that they appear to me not to be citizens of that city, *but to be all priests, to be all ministers and officers of Ceres.* [Italics added.]

The site of the Temple of Persephone is on the grounds now owned by the monastery of the Minorite friars. They prohibit women from viewing it.

I've written before of the Madonna with the female Jesus that I was taken to see in 1964. It is not the only one of its kind, though. The Museum of Castrogiovanni contains a statue of the Goddess Demeter with her infant daughter Persephone in her arms. It stems from the Roman era and was used for centuries by Catholics as their Madonna and Jesus, though the child is obviously a girl. It is the source from which all Italian depictions of the Madonna and Child originate. What is little known is that Persephone was called the Saviour by the continental Greeks. She had a Resurrection. The masculine form of Soter was often used as a feminine noun.

Monte Arsenale, 2,645 feet, is near Castrogiovanni and is considered the real center of Sicily. A stone at Castrogiovanni, near the Temple of Persephone, marks the exact centre of the island, and it is called the "Ombelico di Sicilia"—the umbilical cord of Sicily.

From the *Rocca di Cerere*—the Rock of Ceres—upon which stood the famed Temple of Ceres, the Christians removed every stone, in their attempt to eradicate its memory. But they could not remove this giant white rock in which the cutting of the rock shows where the ancient temple was erected. It is still one of the most legendary and romantic spots in Sicily, framed by the majestic mountains in the background.

Sicily itself has countless ruins of old temples, including ancient tombs and underground catacombs. The latter are vast prehistoric cemeteries cut right into the rock. Some are believed to have been carved by a pre-Sikel troglodyte race. There are cave dwellings and terra cotta sarcophagi, and the lower Empire tombs are similar to the Celtic cromlech, loose altar stones made of slab. The following is an incomplete list of the many ruined temples to be found in Sicily:

1) Temple of Neptune, Messina, built into the back of the church of SS. Annunziata dei Catalani;

2) Temple of Apollo, Taormina, its cella forming the church of Saint Pancrazio;

3) A stylobate of a small temple above the theater in Taormina, to whom it was erected is as yet unknown.

4) Temple of Hadranus, remains at Aderno, known as "the Temple of a thousand dogs."

5) Temple of Minerva, Syracuse, embodied in its Cathedral.

6) Temple of Diana, Syracuse, in the Via Diana.

7) The Olympium, Syracuse, near the Anapo.

8) Temple of Apollo, Syracuse, only the foundations remain, above the Greek theater.

9) Temple of Bacchus, Syracuse, excavated around the first of this century, found near the catacombs of Saint Giovanni.

10) The Adytum, Syracuse, near the Scala Greca.

11) Temple of Ceres and Proserpine, Syracuse, near the Campo Santa believed to be part of the fortifications of Dionysius;

12) Temple of Terranova, the Ancient Gela, which many archaeologists falsely identified with that of Apollo;

13) Temples of Giarratana, the ancient Ceretanum, only remains;

14) Temple of Juno, Girgenti

15) Temple of Concordia, Girgenti

16) Temple of Hercules, Girgenti

17) Temple of Olympian Jove, Girgenti

18) Temple of Castor and Pollux, Girgenti, whose three exquisite remaining columns are still featured in so many photographs

19) Temple of Vulcan, Girgenti, just beyond Castor and Pollux

20) Temple of Aesculapius, Girgenti, in a field just below the other temples.

21) Temple of the Sun, Girgenti, also called the Oratory of Philaris, a beautiful, nearly perfect, building.

22) The Temple of Ceres, on the Rupe Atenea, whose entire cella forms the Church of Saint Biagio

23) Temple of Jupiter Polias under the church of Saint Maria dei Greci;

24) Temple of Olympia Jove or Apollo, Selinunte, this is Temple "G."

25) Temple of Minerva, Selinunte, called Temple "F."

26) Temple of Juno, Selinunte, called Temple "E"

27) Temple of Hercules, the Acropolis, Selinunte, Temple "C"

28) Acropolis, Selinunte, called Temple "B" (still colored).

29) Acropolis, Selinunte, Temple "A"

30) Acropolis, Selinunte, Temple "A"

31) Temple of Hecate, on a further hill in Selinunte, which has a propylaea, the only one in Sicily

32) Temple of Diana, Segeste,

33) Temple of Venus at Eryx (Monte San Giuliano), little left,

34) Temple of Ceres at Enna (Castrogiovanni), only the noble rock formations are left;

35) Temple at Solunto, origin unknown.

36) Greek Temple at Buonfornello, the ancient Himera, visible ruins

37) Temple of Diana, Cefalu, on the Castle rock, considered to be a superb prehistoric house more than a temple.

38) Temple at Tyndaris, a few remains below the convent of the Madonna del Tindaro

39) Temple of Centuripe, Roman, some remains.

40) Temple of Ferale or Heroum, Palazzolo, a rock shrine with many niches and inscriptions.

8

The Healing Power of Plants and Herbs

Modern medicine owes a great deal to medieval Witches' brews. Without the Witches' painstaking pioneering efforts, there would be no twentieth-century wonder drugs. The savage's concoctions evolved into scientific cures. Ancient botany has turned into big business. "Old wives' tales" and "home remedies" now help hubby's health and are mass-produced by million-dollar drug firms. Yesterday's "hogwash" is today's healer. Past "superstitions" have become science's present prescriptions.

Today's psychedelic subculture is a throwback to the Witches' brews of olden days. Mind-blowing and consciousness-expanding drugs, notably peyote and LSD, had their counterpart in the drugs used during the Witches' sabbats. A sixteenth-century work, *Magica Naturis* (natural magic) had a psychedelic recipe which included such ingredients as belladonna, thorn apple, parsley, and the fat of an unbaptized infant. In 1960, Erich-Will Peuckert, a philologist at the University of Göttingen, created an ointment from these substances, successfully substituting kitchen lard in lieu of baby fat. When Professor Peuckert and a friend rubbed their entire bodies with this salve, they fell into a twenty-hour trance and described hallucinations, fantasies, and visions of flying through the air, riding on broomsticks, and participating in a Witches' Sabbat over four hundred years ago. If they had lived during Inquisitional times they would have been burned at the stake, sincerely believing that they had actually done these things.

When Sepp Schwab chopped wood at ten years old, against his parents' wishes, and accidentally hurt his knee, he kept it to himself. After a few days the wound became infected. When his mother noticed it, she called the doctor in alarm. Gangrene had set in and all the doctor could advise, in order to save the boy's life, was amputation of the leg. With great difficulty Mr. and Mrs. Schwab persuaded the doctor to postpone the operation.

In their anguish the father remembered the miraculous cures of a certain shepherd. They contacted him. The shepherd came back with a handful of plants which he cut up into fine pieces, looking like a mass of spinach. Some of the plants the Schwabs recognized as the common nettle, plantain, and watercress. He placed this on the boy's diseased knee. That night the boy's fever began to abate. When the doctor removed the bandage next morning he saw that the swelling had stopped. He permitted the parents to continue with the

The Healing Power of Plants and Herbs 163

treatment. After the second treatment the doctor said that an amputation would no longer be necessary.

Sepp Schwab's best friend, Richard Willstätter, observed all these transactions with fascination. It made an idelible impression on his mind, one that he never forgot. He knew that he had witnessed a secret of nature. He studied chemistry at Munich University. Twelve years later he was appointed a professor at Zurich. He specialized in biochemistry of plants and in 1930 published his findings. He discovered chlorophyll, the coloring matter of plants. In 1932 he was awarded the Nobel Prize for his discoveries.

Dr. Willstätter's theory was that the sun was the source of all life. Only plants can create life from "dead" matter, and each is itself a miniature chemical factory. When the sun's rays hit the plant, its carbon dioxide particles yield material which is converted into carbohydrates. With the aid of chlorophyll and the sun, from this is formed carbonic acid and later starch. One of the most fascinating discoveries of Dr. Willstätter and the host of other researchers into this field was that the biochemical properties of the chlorophyll molecule was almost identical to the red blood pigment, hemoglobin. Chlorophyll had the ability to destroy bacteria on the living tissue of a sick person (though it did not do this in a test tube). Without knowing the reasons why, and certainly unable to scientifically explain how it worked, the herbal concoction of the peasant, handed down to him from generation to generation, a "home remedy," paved the way for a great discovery in modern medicine.

Mahatma Gandhi was the world's most successful exponent of passive resistance and nonviolence, inspiration for the late Dr. Martin Luther King's own use of these tactics in gaining full civil rights. One of the little known facts about Gandhi was that he habitually dipped the Indian plant, rauwolfia, into his tea for its calming effect. For over thirty centuries African and Indian peoples chewed the roots of this plant to alleviate such things as depression, tension, anxiety, nervous upset, and irritability. Another name for this plant is snakeroot. When scientists in 1931 began to take a serious interest in this plant (known to herbalists for thousands of years), it wasn't until twenty-one years later that they discovered the secret that made this herb tick. It was found in the root and identified as reserpine. This is the basis for all of our current tranquilizer drugs. As one drug company executive put it, "We finally figured that one million Indians couldn't be wrong."

For centuries local Wise men and Wise women, Witches, well versed in the healing properties of plants and herbs, made a salve out of the decaying leaves of the hyssop plant. Applied to various wounds and sores, the ailment healed, the patient got better, the Witch's reputation as a "miracle worker" was assured. Not the least of these cures involved people suffering from the dreaded venereal diseases. The Gospel of St. John (19:28–29) says, "After this, Jesus knowing that all things were now accomplished, that the scripture might be fulfilled, saith, I thirst. Now there was set a vessel full of vinegar: and they filled a sponge with vinegar, and put it upon hyssop, and put it to his mouth." Hyssop became a symbol of purification from sin, and it was to be proven a medically purifying force centuries later.

In 1929, Dr. Alexander Fleming, a Scot, discovered by accident that certain bacterial cultures had been contaminated by a mold which slowed down their growth. In his laboratory he isolated this antibacterial substance and found that it was active against disease-producing bacteria called *streptococci, staphylococci,* and *pneumococci*. At the beginning of World War II, research into this increased and a group of British scientists discovered that this antibacterial agent was just as active in a living body as it was in a test tube. In 1943 this substance was isolated, proven, and made available to the public. In 1944 Dr. Fleming was knighted and in the following year shared the Nobel Prize in medicine with his collaborators, Dr. Howard W. Florey and Dr. Ernst Boris Chain (a refugee from Hitler's Germany). Prior to all this it was a Swedish scientist, Westling, who was the first to isolate this fungus (mold) from the decaying leaves of the blue labiate hyssop. And what was this remarkable Nobel Prize-winning discovery? Penicillin.

During the twelfth century there existed a remarkable woman, Hildegard von Bingen, who was the abbess of a nunnery. In that superstition-ridden pre-Pasteur period, Hildegard insisted that all of her nuns maintain the strictest of hygienic habits at a time when the body was despised and the religious were told not to concern themselves with corporal or worldly matters. She had running water installed in all the convent cells and instructed the nuns to brush their teeth and to attend chapel always well groomed. She truly practiced the concept "cleanliness is next to godliness." Hildegard wrote, "When God looked into the face of the man he had created he recognized all the works of his creation in this same pure form."

Keenly observant, Hildegard recorded all her insights into a work called *Physica*. Without knowing it, she had formulated an antibiotic pharmacy long before scientists ever knew, let alone proved, that such things as microbes, bacteria, and biotics existed. For a treatment of a venereal disease that had symptoms similar to leprosy, she prescribed a bath prepared from agrimony and hyssop—the same hyssop that the Levites used to cure a disease called *cara-at* during the time of Moses—the same hyssop that provided the mold from which penicillin was discovered. Other ingredients included an extract of ground ivy and blood: specifically, menstrual blood. Another remedy was a combination of chicken fat mixed with chicken manure. Today scientists would recognize in this a concoction of antibiotics.

Hildegard lists a variety of fungi in her *Physica:* Fungus from the beech tree was good against stomach cold and gastritis; from the willow good against diseases of the lungs and spleen, and scurf; from the hazelnut trees a treatment against worms. The fungus from rotting leaves was good for the glands. Hildegard used the moss from old roofs and trees and decaying wood as a treatment for inflammatory conditions, fevers, and forms of tuberculosis. Like the Peruvians and Japanese, of whom she knew nothing, she prescribed the bark of the peach tree for bad breath and shingles. She warned that certain wild berries could be harmful to some people, causing skin reactions, such as the strawberry. She was totally familiar with the therapeutic value in some soils, and in using them stressed that one soil was good for one condition but not necessarily good for another—that the earth beneath the various trees all had different properties— the earth beneath the lime tree was good for gout, while that found under the maple cured a nose cold.

One of the greatest scientific researchers into the effectiveness of ancient herbals is Professor Arrien Gerhard Winter of Bonn. Winter and his assistants searched out every known variety of plant and herb, did countless laboratory tests, and proved that the old books on herbs, notably the *Book of Herbs* by Hieronymus Bosch and another by Matthiolus, published during the sixteenth century, had to be reevaluated. Professor Winter took every plant and herb listed in the Index of Matthiolus's work and experimented with them, one by one. He discovered that the healing merits given to one herb wasn't restricted to just that herb but applied to all those that belonged to this same family group.

The results of all these investigations showed that 65 percent of the herbal remedies of the Middle Ages and Renaissance had antibiotic activity. Later researches showed that out of 1,248 plants studied and analyzed, at least 29.5 percent of them were antibiotically active. Later research by E. M. Osborm, who by 1943 had studied 2,300 species of plants, followed by 450 new ones by Atkinson and Rainsford, and then another 231 by Hayes by the end of 1947—a total of 2981 plants and herbs altogether—confirmed these findings.

When in 1952 Winter became director of the Botanical Division of the House of Madaus (named after Dr. Gerhard Madaus, a pioneer researcher into the study of herbs and plants since 1919, and head of the drug firm bearing his name), he decided to implement his botanical knowledge in the treatment of patients. In collaboration with university and private clinics Dr. Winter often used nasturtium cress in his treatments, to the amusement and skepticism of his medical colleagues. It saved the life of a mother of four children suffering from an infection of the renal pelvis, a case that prohibited operation. He borrowed another witches'-brew formula in applying a poultice of mustard seeds and horse radish, used in the past to treat pneumonia, pleurisy, tonsillitis, and even meningitis. The doctors were surprised to see that the mustard oil was absorbed by the skin into the body, acted as an antibiotic agent, and finally excreted in the urine. Critics scoffed at and ridiculed Winter's treatments, saying he was "going back to the Middle Ages."

"This is not a retrograde step," Dr. Winter said. "The physician of the Middle Ages treated diseases of which he did not know the cause with plants of which he did not know the ingredients. The doctor of our time is safeguarded against their mistakes. He treats known diseases with known remedies. That is a great and fundamental difference. In the Middle Ages people groped in the dark, but we have advanced to such an extent that, with our knowledge, we can use the tools of the past with purpose and direction. As we find the tools to be of good quality, our therapy will be good."

The work of Dr. Winter is too extensive to go into here, but he has confirmed the wisdom of the ancient occultists, herbalists, witches, and shamans. Without scientific apparatus, and considering the limited and restricted sphere in which they functioned, their reputation as healers is well deserved.

One of the most important botanical researchers was the Roman physician, Dioscorides, born about A.D. 64. His *De Materia Medica* describes and illustrates over five hundred herbs and plants, and this manuscript has been copied and recopied for at least seventeen centuries. It became the basis for all other such herbals. In fact, if a plant or herb was not listed therein it was very difficult for it to obtain recognition as a healing agent. When printing began in fifteenth-century Europe, herbals were very popular, though most were plagiarisms of Dioscorides. In the sixteenth century some new ones of value appeared, notably *The History of Plants* by Valerius Cordus, published in Prussia in 1561.

Although ancient texts on botany exist, including an Egyptian papyrus of about 1600 B.C. containing a list of drug plants and their uses, and an Assyrian one of about 700 B.C., plus the works of Hippocrates (460 and 370 B.C.), the real beginnings of botanical science lies in the works of Aristotle (384–322 B.C.) and Theophrastus (370–287 B.C.). Both were pupils of Plato. Because only fragments of Aristotle's botanical writings are extant, it is his pupil and colleague Theophrastus who is called the father of botany. He succeeded Aristotle as head of the Lyceum in Athens, inheriting Aristotle's garden, which had about 450 species of herbs and plants. He wrote two books which proved that he was an astute observer and ecologist, noted the relationship and communities of plants found together in grasslands, woodlands, and marshes, and recorded the healing properties of various plants gained from his experiences with the armies of Alexander the Great. Yet, in spite of occasional works on the subject, Theophrastus had no botanical descendants for almost eighteen centuries. Those who possessed this knowledge passed it on from generation to generation, becoming the guardians of family secrets and jealously withheld information, and these were the village Wise men and Wise women, wizards, witches, and wonder-workers.

For over five thousand years garlic has been used to treat everything from worms to ague, old age, asthma, bacteria, coughs, diarrhea, diabetes, dyspepsia, fevers, sciatica—name it! Slave-builders of the great pyramid Cheops were fed garlic daily. The Vikings and Phoenicians carried huge amounts of it on their sea voyages. When the wandering Israelites left Egypt they bemoaned the fact that garlic was no longer easily obtained. Dioscorides, the physician and botanist who accompanied the Roman armies as their official physician, prescribed garlic for all lung and intestinal disorders. Hippocrates, the "father of medicine," advocated garlic as a laxative and diuretic. Muhammad claimed that when "garlic is applied on the sting of the scorpion or the bite of the viper it produces favorable results." When the bubonic plagues raged throughout Europe during the Middle Ages, most of the people who ate their daily quotient of garlic were not infected.

In the book *Euterpe—Concerning the History of Egypt*, written about 450 B.C., the Greek historian Herodotus writes, "There is an inscription inside the pyramid which is written in Egyptian characters. It tells us of the quantity of radishes, onions, and garlic that were consumed by the workers building the pyramids. I remember most exactly that the interpreter who deciphered the inscription for me remarked that the sum of money spent on these items would amount to 1,600 talents of silver."

Broken down over the twenty-year period it took to build the Cheops pyramid, that comes to the equivalent of £1,323,804, as Helmuth M. Boettcher calculated in his book *Wonder Drugs*. In American dollars, the Egyptians spent something like $3,900,000 to feed onions, garlic, and radishes, to their 360,000 pyramid workers.

What is the scientific evidence to justify the expenditure of so much money? Is there any real *proven*

The Healing Power of Plants and Herbs

value, medically speaking, in radishes, onions, and garlic? In 1947, researchers G. Ivanovics and St. Horvath isolated a water-soluble substance from radish seeds, called Raphanin, and demonstrated that it was an antibiotic active against both gram-positive and gram-negative microbes. The same antibiotic substances were also discovered in the onion and the garlic. Later researchers discovered a property called *allicin*, an antibiotically active principle found in the oil of garlic. Painstaking experiments showed that *allicin* was active against bacteria causing conjunctivitis, sepsis, typhoid, tuberculosis, cholera, and skin fungus. Furthermore, these scientists proved that far from being superstitious nonsense, a milligram of *allicin* had the same effect as twenty-five units of penicillin. The statement that those who ate their daily quotient of garlic during the bubonic plague escaped infection is now backed up by scientific research. Research into the lowly much-maligned onion family is continuing, and recently two more substances that are antibiotically active have been discovered: *garlicin* and *allistatin*.

When the sorceress Circe gave the men of Odysseus a magic potion that turned them into pigs, the God Hermes comes to his assistance with a medicinal plant and this warning in Homer's tale of Odysseus's voyage:

> In vain she endeavours to transform you;
> The virtue of this medicinal plant stands
> against her...

Then Homer proceeds to describe this plant:

> Its roots were black and milky white
> flowered the blossom.
> Moly it is named by the gods...

Just what was this miracle plant called *moly*? It is mentioned and identified by Theophrastus. It is a form of mountain leek, in the onion family. It grew on ground considered sacred by the ancient Greeks. During the Renaissance when there was a revival of interest and study of the ancient Greek literature, the Italian botanists determined to rediscover the moly. It was placed in the *Allium* family. Two hundred years later it was classified by Linnaeus as *allium magicum* or *Allium moly*. Because the *Allium* family possessed such curative powers (garlic, onions, leeks, moly), there grew up all sorts of magical, mystical, and supernatural myths around these herbs. One of these was the use of garlic as a protection against vampires and werewolves. In Germany the onion was called *Siegwurz* (*sieg*, "victory"; *wurz*, "root") and *Allermannsharnisch* (*Allermann*, "all and sundry"; *Harnisch*, "to harness"). In this you can see the complete trust the Germans had in the *Allium* family.

In my book *Curses In Verses* I write about a formula for curing the common cold handed down to me from my father whose mother was a Sicilian *strega* and reader of the old *Tarrochi* cards:

>Onions and sugar boil
>   Into a syrup thick
>Common cold this will foil
>   Witches' old magick trick.
>Chop in pieces garlic
>   Place into a small sack,
>The inhaled fumes will lick,
>   coughs . . . keeping health intact.
>From onions science found
>   *Alium cepa* . . . name

The Healing Power of Plants and Herbs

    Cold cure grown in the ground,
        Gaining Witches their fame.
    And don't forget the Jews,
        Whose most famous cure-all,
    Is happy home He-brews
        Chicken broth for all!

9

Mother Shipton: Magnificent Seeress

Mother Shipton, was born in July, 1488, near the Dropping Well, Knaresborough, Yorkshire, England. Her mother's name was Agatha Southill. Her father was unknown. She was named Ursula. Legend has it that her father was not mortal and that he rewarded his mistress with the powers of healing or harming, raising storms, and clairvoyance. Compare this with the powers given to Witches by the Goddess as outlined in *Aradia*. Anyway, one thing is certain: Her circumstances changed for the better. Her many long disappearances aroused curiosity and constant questions. (There is no recorded proof that she belonged to a coven, but if she did that would help give one explanation for these disappearances.) Exasperated with being pestered for answers, it is said that she "called up the wind" and blew all of them out of

Mother Shipton: Magnificent Seeress   175

their own homes. She was brought before the local magistrates on a charge of being a Witch. Nothing came of it.

It wasn't long after the birth of Ursula that Agatha retired into a convent, where she died. Ursula was raised by a parish nurse. In school she proved to be brilliant, a fast learner. But her appearance made her the butt of cruel jokes. Ungainly, homely, with a crooked nose, bulging eyes, big bones, and bowlegs, she was not without resources. Her tormentors were kicked, pinched, and punched by seemingly invisible hands and feet. Unable to handle this kind of thing, the school authorities dismissed her. There is no record that she continued her formal education after that.

Her looks must have improved somewhat, because at the age of twenty-four she married Tobias Shipton. History records nothing more about him. But Ursula Shipton's amazing prophetic ability was already known. In an old book called *The Life of Mother Shipton,* the author writes, "Never a day passed wherein she did not relate something remarkable, and that required the most serious consideration. People flocked to her from far and near, her fame was so great. They went to her of all sorts, both old and young, rich and poor, especially young maidens, to be resolved of their doubts relating to things to come; and all returned wonderfully satisfied in the explanations she gave to their questions."

While doing research on two books in the New York Public Library, I came across a very old, rare book, *Mother Shipton,* on microfilm, published in 1865. The first edition of this work was published in 1641 and another in 1645. Both rare editions are now in the Library's reference department. The following verse is most timely today, what with the now generation, unisex clothes, women's liberation, longhaired men and shorthaired women, birth control pills, and antimarriage views of many young people, and the revolution in dress, manners, and morals:

> And now a word in uncouth rhyme
>   Of what shall be in future time
> For in these wondrous far off days
>   The women shall adopt a craze,
> To dress like men and trousers wear,
>   And cut off all their locks of hair.
> They'll ride astride with brazen brow,
>   As witches do on broomsticks now,
> The love shall die and marriage cease,
>   And nations wane as babes decrease
> And wives shall fondle cats and dogs,
>   And men live much the same as hogs,
> Just for food and lust.

This verse evokes so many emotional memories. How often have you read about divorcing couples desperately fighting in court over the possession of their pets, cats and dogs? The use of the word *hog* is similar to the *pig* used by revolutionary groups to describe police and the despised "establishment." The latter also use it to describe "hippies" as "living like pigs." And the pantsuits for women have now come full circle with the fad of hot pants.

Among the many of Mother Shipton's prophecies that have come true are the following:

Carriages without horses shall go,
Disaster fill the world with woe.

Mother Shipton: Magnificent Seeress

(Trains, automobiles, buses etc.)
The states shall lock in fiercest strife,
And seek to take each other's life,
When North shall thus divide the South.
(The Civil War in the United States)
Beneath the water men shall walk, shall ride, shall sleep
Shall even talk, and in the air men shall be seen,
In white, in black, in green.

(Submarines, airplanes, rocket ships, satellite TV, etc.)
Mother Shipton accurately predicted the two world wars as follows:

The time will come when seas of blood,
Shall mingle with a greater flood;
Great noise there shall be heard,
Great shouts and cries,
And seas shall thunder louder than the skies,
Then shall three Lions fight with three,
Joy to the people, and honor to the King.
When pictures look alive with movements free,
When ships like fishes swim beneath the sea,
When men outstripping birds can soar the sky,
Then half the world deep drenched in blood shall die!

An analysis of the above reveals her description of the bloody sea battles in both the Atlantic and the Pacific (and lesser waterways) during both wars; the "great noise" of the cannons, torpedo charges, bombs; the "three lions"—America, England, and France—fighting against the Axis alliance of Germany, Italy, and Japan during World War II. She again describes submarines and airplanes. Her "when pictures look alive with movements free" is a perfect prophecy of the worldwide multibillion-dollar motion-picture industry and television. The next verse includes a specific date:

> In 1936 build houses with straw and sticks.
>   For then mighty wars shall be planned,
> And fire and sword shall sweep the land.

This accurately foretells the building of prefabricated houses and the threatening war-storms emanating from Germany in 1936. It could also be allegorical in the sense that Chamberlain and others built "straw houses" in the belief and acceptance of Hitler's "good intentions." Here are a few more of her prophetic verses with commentary:

> Around the earth thought shall fly,
> In a twinkling of an eye.
> (Morse Code, S.O.S., Radio, TV, Radar, teletype, Satellite etc.)
> Over a wild and stormy sea, shall a noble man sail,
>   Who to find will not fail,
> A new and fair country; from whence he will
>   bring an herb and root
> That all men shall suit.
>   And please both the plowman and the king,
> And let them take no more than measure,
>   Both shall have the even pleasure,
> In bell and brain.

In 1586 Sir Francis Drake and Sir Walter Raleigh each brought to England the first tobacco and potatoes ever seen there. They got this from Indians in Virginia. The first part of this verse could apply also to the first voyage of Columbus. The herb is tobacco. The root is the potato.

Mother Shipton's prophecy of the great London fire and its effects on the populace of the time is recorded in the Harleian Manuscripts, published by the Royal Society of Antiquaries, and now in the British Museum. An eyewitness who accompanied the Duke of York says that they were hindered in stopping the flames by the passive resignation of the people who refused to try and stop it. Mother Shipton had written:

> When fate to England shall restore
> A king to reign as heretofore,
> Great death in London shall be though,
> And many houses be laid low.

There were two other prophecies about this fire. One was written before her time and the other one afterwards. The *London Saturday Journal* of March 12, 1842, published both of them with this comment: "An absurd report is gaining ground among the weak-minded, that London will be destroyed by an earthquake on the 17th of March, or St. Patrick's day. This rumour is founded on the following ancient prophecies: one professing to be pronounced in the year 1203; the other, by Dr. Dee the astrologer, in 1598:

> In eighteen hundred and forty-two
> Four things the sun shall view:
> London's rich and famous town
> Hungry earth shall swallow down,
> Storm and rain in France shall be,
> Till every river runs a sea.

> Spain shall be rent in twain,
> And famine waste the land again.
> So say I, the Monk of Dree,
> In the twelve hundred year and three.

This prophecy is in the Harleian Collection as is the following one. Because of the panic that it caused, officials denied that these prophecies existed. Here's the one by Dr. Dee:

> The Lord have mercy on you all.
> Prepare yourselves for dreadful fall
> Of house and land and human soul—
> The measure of your sins is full.
> In the year one, eight and forty-two,
> Of the year that is so new;
> In the third month of that sixteen,
> It may be a day or two between—
> Perhaps you'll soon be stiff and cold.
> Dear Christian, be not stout and bold—
> The mighty, kingly-proud will see
> This comes to pass as my name's Dee.

Mother Shipton lived during the reign of King Henry VIII, and her utterances were a prophetic catalogue of all the calamities and catastrophes of the period. Twenty years before St. Paul's steeple was destroyed by fire (June, 1561), she had written, "Great London's triumphant spire, shall be consumed with flames of fire." At the urging of the Abbot of Beverly, for whom she had made so many accurate forecasts, she rendered in verse a long-range prophetic view of the coming centuries. One of her last lines was, "The world then to an end shall come, in nineteen hundred and ninety-nine."

One of the most famous of Mother Shipton's prophecies concerned Cardinal Wolsey. In the book *Mother Shipton Investigated* by W. H. Harrison (1881), he quotes extensively from an earlier work, *Mother Shipton and Nixon's Prophecies* by S. Baker (1797). In both is the following:

"When Cardinal Wolsey intended to remove his residence to York, Mother Shipton announced that he would never reach the city. The Cardinal sent three lords of his retinue in disguise to inquire whether she had made such a prediction, and to threaten her if she persisted in it. She was then living in a village called Dring Houses, a mile to the west of the city. The retainees, led by a guide named Beasly, knocked at her door.

"Come in, Mr. Beasly, and three noble lords with you," said Mother Shipton.

She then treated them civilly, by setting oatcakes and ale before them.

"You gave out," said they, "the Cardinal Wolsey should never see York."

"No," she replied, "I said he might see it, but never come to it."

They responded, "When he does come he'll surely burn thee."

"If this burn," said Reverent Mother, "so shall I."

She then cast her linen handkerchief into the fire, allowed it to remain in the flames a quarter of an hour, and took it out unsinged.

One of her awe-stricken visitors then asked what she thought of him. She answered:

"The time will come, Lord, when you shall be as low as I am, and that is low indeed."

This was judged to be verified when Thomas Lord Cromwell was beheaded.

Cardinal Wolsey, on his arrival at Cawood, ascended the castle tower, and while viewing York, eight miles off, vowed he would burn the witch when he reached there. But ere he descended the stairs, a message from the King demanded his presence forthwith, and while on his journey to London he was taken ill and died at Leicester.

Mother Shipton's prophecy proved correct.

William Lilly, the famous astrologer, published his book *A Collection of Ancient and Modern Prophecies* in 1645 with this annotation: "Shipton's Prophecies, after the most exact copy." He discovered that out of twenty prophecies he studied, at least sixteen of them were fulfilled. Some of these included the beheading of the Duke of Suffolk; that of Lord Percy, "his head was stolen and carried into France"; the fire and flood that affected the Trinity Church and Ouse Bridge. Another one that refers to the London fire of 1666 was: "And after that a ship come sailing up the Thames till it come against London, and the Master of the ship shall weep, and the marriners shall ask him why he weepeth, being he hath made so good a voyage, and he shall say: Ah, what a goodly citie that was, none in the world comparable to it, and now there is scarce left any house that can let is have drink for our money."

S. Baker, commenting on this prophecy about the great fire, said, ". . . which left not one house between

Mother Shipton: Magnificent Seeress

the Tower and the Temple. This fire, at all events, occurred long after Mother Shipton's death and the publication of her alledged prophecy."

In the book *The Story of Prophecy* by Henry James Forman, he writes, "Every land, it would appear, has its own peculiar style for prophecies. The British, English as well as Scottish, affects an oracular strain that is half riddle, half epigram. 'Shooe your horse in the quicke, and you shall doe well.' Or, 'When Hempe is spun, England's done.' Rede this riddle, current in Tudor times, and it tells you that with the passing of the sovereigns Henry, Edward, Mary and Philip, and Elizabeth, England will be no more England, or not the same England." True, in a sense; for with the coming of Elizabeth's successor, James I, England and Scotland were united in Britain. Indeed another version of the distich, runs, "When Hempe is come and gone Scotland and England shall be one."

The earlier-mentioned guide Beasly, after having witnessed Mother Shipton's prophecy of Cardinal Wolsey come true, asked her to make others for him. "Master," said she, "before the Owes Bridge and Trinitie Church meet, they shall build on the day, and it shall fall in the night, until they get the highest stone of Trinitie Church, to be the lowest stone of Owes Bridge, then the day shall come when the North shall rue it wondrous sore, but the South shall rue it forevermore. When Hares kinle on cold harth stones, and Lads shall marry Ladys, and bring them home, then shall you have a year of pyning hungar, and then a dearth without Corne. A woful day shall be seen in England, a King and Queene, the first coming of the King of Scots shall be at Holgate Towne, but he shall not come through the barre, and when the King of the North shall be at London Bridge, and a Windmill shall be set on a Tower, and an Elm-tree shall lye at every mans doore at that time women shall weare great hats and great bands, and when there is a Lord Major at Yorke let him beware of a stab. When two Knights shall fall out in the castle yard, they shall bee kindly all their lives after; When Calton Hagge hath borne seven yeares Crops of Corne, seven years after you heare newes, there shall two Judges goe in and out at Mungate barre.

> Then Warres shall begin in the spring,
> Much woe to England bring,
> Then shall the Ladys cry well-away,
> That ever we liv'd to see this day.

Author Forman comments, "As a specimen of the content, rather than as important prophecy, the quotation illustrates the style England loved in its vaticination. There is considerably more of the same. Lilly surveyed twenty of those prophecies and found sixteen of them fulfilled by 1654. For instance, the Duke of Suffolk had duly been beheaded; Lord Percy, likewise, and 'his head was stolen and carried into France.' A tempest and a flood carried out the prophecy concerning Trinity Church and the Ouse Bridge, and so on."

Two centuries before Mother Shipton was born "Friar Bacon" had made predictions concerning "carriages without horses." Roger Bacon died in 1292. His fellow monks put him in jail thinking that it was a safer place than the monastery. In his alchemical laboratory he discovered gunpowder. In the book *Things Not Generally Known,* Volume VI, by John Timbs, F.S.A., published in 1880, Bacon is quoted as writing that "en-

Mother Shipton: Magnificent Seeress

gines of navigation may be made without seamen, so that the greatest river and sea ships, with only one man to steer them, may sail swifter than if they were fully manned. Moreover, chariots may be made so as to be moved with incalculable force without any beast drawing them. . . . And such things might be made to infinity, as, for instance, bridges to traverse rivers without pillars or any buttress."

Mother Shipton was a witch in the oldest, truest sense, though there is no record that she belonged to any coven or worshipped the old gods and goddesses. She undoubtedly perfected her divinatory powers as an overcompensation for her ungainly appearance. In time her remarkable accurate prophecies gained her attention—her abilities won out—her appearance went totally unnoticed. From a mercilessly ridiculed, ugly child she rose to the position of a revered adult. Most remarkable of all is the fact that she was so well known at a time when even a suggestion of any kind of psychic ability would be enough to have her burned at the stake, as Cardinal Wolsey threatened to do. Yet she outlived them all, and what's more, told them that she would.

The incident of the handkerchief thrown into the fire and taken out fifteen minutes later without even a singe is not necessarily miraculous. Modern magicians are able to easily duplicate this feat. Mother Shipton undoubtedly had a knowledge of herbs and chemicals and it's possible the handkerchief was chemically treated. This bit of "stage magic" or showmanship in no way detracts from what she said—shortly proven accurate in every detail.

Occult aficionados collect the prophecies of Mother Shipton as well as those of Lilly, Merlin, Bede, Berlington, and Thomas the Rhymer. Scholars have established that the latter existed some time in the thirteenth century, between 1220 and 1297. He was probably a vassal in the employ of the Earl of March. In the book *The Romance and Prophecies of Thomas of Erceldoune,* edited by J. A. H. Murray, published in 1875, it says that while he was visiting the Castle of Dunbar, the Earl of March "interrogated him in the jocular manner which he was wont to assume with the Rymour, what another day was to bring forth."

Sighing heavily, Thomas the Rhymer said, "Alas for tomorrow, a day of calamity and misery! Before the twelfth hour shall be heard a blast so vehement that it shall exceed all those that have yet been heard in Scotland: a blast which shall strike the nations with amazement, shall confound those who hear it, shall humble what is lofty, and what is unbending shall level to the ground."

The Earl of March laughed, pooh-poohing Thomas's dire warnings. However, at twelve noon, just when the Earl was to begin dinner, a messenger galloped in announcing the death of King Alexander III, who had been hurled over a cliff at Kinghorn.

In *The History of the Church of Scotland,* Archbishop Spottiswood (1565–1639) discusses the prophecies of Thomas the Rhymer, saying that they "may be justly admired, having foretold, to many ages before, the union of England and Scotland, in the ninth degree of the Bruce's blood, with the succession of Bruce himself to the crown, being yet a child, and other divers particulars which the event hath ratified and made good."

Thomas the Rhymer's prophecy to the Earl of Mars was a detailed one which took three hundred years to be fulfilled, and they were—to the letter. The Earl of

Mother Shipton: Magnificent Seeress

Mars was made Regent of Scotland in 1571, and guardian of James I, whose cradle belonged to the family. His unfinished palace at Stirling became known as "Marr's Work." He was defeated in the rebellion of 1715. He lost his title and his lands. His grandson, James Francis's wife, was burned at Alloa Tower. She left three children, all born blind. When George IV visited Scotland in 1822, he restored the titles and lands lost by those who had embraced the Stuart cause, including the earldom to the Erskine of Mar. He became known as the Earl of Mar and Kelly. His wife was never presented at Court, but by accident she met Queen Victoria at Stirling Castle. The latter liked her and embraced her, thus fulfilling Thomas the Rhymer's prophecy, "the many who knew the family in its days of deepest depression, have lived to see 'the weird dreed out, and the doom of Mar ended.'"

The above, very abbreviated data will best be understood by Thomas the Rhymer's prophecy as it appeared in the book *Family Romance* by Sir Bernard Burke:

> Proud Chief of Mar: Thou shalt be raised higher, until thou sittest in the place of King. Thou shall rule and destroy, and thy work be after thy name; but thy work shall be the emblem of thy house, and shall teach mankind, that he who cruelly and haughtily raiseth himself upon the ruins of the holy cannot prosper. Thy work shall be cursed and shall never be finished. But thou shalt have riches and greatness, and shalt be true to thy soverign and shalt raise his banner in the field of blood. Then, when thou seemest to be highest—when thy power is mightiest, then shall

come thy fall; low shall be thy head among the nobles of thy people. Deep shall be thy moan among the children of dool (sorrow). Thy lands shall be given to strangers; and thy titles shall lie among the dead. The branch that springs from thee shall see his dwelling burnt, in which a King is nursed—his wife a sacrifice in that same flame; his children numerous, but of little honor; and three born and grown who shall never see the light: Yet shall thine ancient tower stand; for the brave and the true cannot wholly be forsaken. Thou proud head and daggered hand must dree thy weird, until horses shall be stabled in thy hall, and a weaver shall throw his shuttle in thy chamber of state. Thine ancient tower, a woman's dower, shall be a ruin and a beacon, until an ash sapling shall spring from its topmost stone. Then shall thy sorrows be ended, and the sunshine of royalty shall beam on thee once more. Thine honors shall be restored; the kiss of peace shall be given to thy Countess, though she seek it not, and the days of peace shall return to thee and thine. The line of Mars shall be broken; but not until its honors are doubled and its doom ended.

Besides Thomas the Rhymer, there are many lesser known Scottish seers, such as those published in a book called *The Prophecies of the Brahan Seer* by Coinneach (or Kenneth) Odhar, famed local prophet who so angered Lady Seaforth that she had him thrown into a barrel of burning tar. Yet before he died, Coinneach made the following prophecy which in time all came true:

I see into the far future, and I read the doom of the race of my oppressors. The long-descended line of Seaforth will, ere many generations have passed, end in extinction and in sorrow. I see a chief, the last of his house, both deaf and dumb. He will be the father of four fair sons, all of whom he will follow to the tomb. He will live careworn and die mourning, knowing that the honors of his line are to be extinguished forever, and that no future chief of the Mackenzies shall bear rule at Brahan or in Kintail. After lamenting over the last and most promising of his sons, he himself shall sink into the grave, and the remnant of his possessions shall be inherited by a white-coifed (or white-hooded) lassie from the East, and she is to kill her sister. And as a sign by which it may be known that these things are coming to pass, there shall be four great lairds in the days of the last deaf and dumb Seaforth—Gairloch, Chisholm, Grant and Raasay—of whom one shall be buck-toothed, another hare-lipped, another half-witted, and the fourth a stammerer. Chiefs distinguished by these personal marks shall be the allies and neighbors of the last Seaforth: and when he looks around him and sees them, he may know that his sons are doomed to death, that his broad lands shall pass away to the stranger, and that his race shall come to an end.

After an outbreak of scarlet fever, Lord Seaforth did become deaf and dumb. He sired six daughters and four sons—as in the prophecy. All of them were afflicted as the prophecy foretold: One buck-toothed, one hare-lipped, one half-witted, the other a stammerer. They all died before him. His eldest daughter had married Admiral Hood, stationed in the West Indies. When he died she returned home and later married a man named Stewart who took the last name of MacKenzie, since all of the male heirs had died. The property was passing into other hands. Her youngest sister, Caroline Mackenzie, was killed in an accident. Her carriage was overthrown while riding because something had frightened the horses. One by one all these prophecies were fulfilled.

Though Mother Shipton also gave out many personal prophecies, and long-range ones, her most famous deal with future world events. The most often-quoted one is the following:

> Carriages without horses shall go,
> And accidents fill the world with woe,
> Around the earth thoughts shall fly
> In the twinkling of an eye;
> The world upside down shall be,
> And gold be found at the root of a tree.
> Through hills man shall ride,
> And no horse be at his side.
> Under water men shall walk,
> Shall ride, shall sleep, shall talk.
> In the air men shall be seen
> In white, in black, in green;
> Iron in the water shall float,
> As easily as a wooden boat.
> Gold shall be found and shown
> In a land that's not now known.
> Fire and water shall wonders do,
> England shall at last admit a foe.

The world to an end shall come
In eighteen hundred and eighty one.

There is a dispute as to whether that last date is 1881, which would be untrue, or 1981, which remains to be seen. The latter seems more plausible (though I personally don't believe it), what with the atomic-hydrogen bombs and other mass death-dealing weapons stockpiled all over the world. However, end of the world or not, it may presage World War III. Every other prediction in the above has come to pass, written nearly four hundred years ago.

Forman, in his *Story of Prophecy*, writes:

Many other prophecies are likewise attributed to her, and even if half of them are true, her understanding surely was, as her biographer describes it, "extraordinary,"—especially if she really existed. As to that, present-day scholarship more and more inclines to the view that there is perhaps no legendary figure but had its prototype in fact. In Mother Shipton's case, at all events, the legend was so powerful that for more than two hundred years it figured prominently in pamphlets and almanacs, and it persists even to this day. Baker declares that she foretold the hour of her own death and departed this life "with much serenity, A.D. 1561, when upwards of seventy years of age." Between the villages of Clifton and Skipton a monument was said to have been erected to her bearing this epitaph:

Here ly's she who never ly'd,
Whose skill often has been try'd,

> Her prophecies shall still survive,
> And ever keep her name alive,

In the book *Witchcraft: The Sixth Sense,* Justine Glass writes, "The Wise Ones—the Wicca—no doubt assisted in the rites of the dolmen and the Rollright circle. The Old Religion has left its mark in the place-names of the country around the stones: Shipton-under-Wychwood—where the famous Wise woman, Mother Shipton, lived—and the forest of Wychwood. 'Wych' is a modified form of spelling of 'witch' or 'Wicca'; the long long history of the cult, echoes in these names as well as in the tradition of the meeting places, all over the country."

10

The Search for Sator

```
S A T O R
A R E P O
T E N E T
O P E R A
R O T A S
```

Hundreds of books on the occult, Witchcraft, and Satanism have used the magic square above, advocated as a charm against disease and death by fire. What is not generally known is that the Sator charm has an ancient history. From 1931 to 1933 Professor Rostovtseff and his Yale University team of archaeologists were excavaying Roman ruins at Dura, called "the Pompeii of the desert," on the Euphrates River. They found one wall that had the above inscription made with red ocher. The writing was Roman, and it was placed in the third century A.D. The one difference was that the word *rotas* was at the top instead of *sator*.

In 1926 Felix Grosser, of Chemnitz, Germany, offered the theory that twenty-one of the twenty-five letters of the Sator square could be arranged as follows:

P
A
T
E
R
PATERNOSTER
O
S
T
E
R

This left two A's and two O's which could be added at the tips of the cross, symbolizing the Alpha and the Omega —the beginning and the end. Grosser attributed to Sator a Christian symbolism. And the word *tenet* forms a cross. It's interesting to note that all of the investigators into Sator were Judeo-Christians. What gave credence to their belief is the fact that so many old Christian Churches had Sator inscribed on them.

When Professor Matteo della Corte, director of Pompeii excavations, declared that he had found Sator on one of the Pompeii columns and that one of his colleagues had found one ten years earlier, this was entered into his notebook on October 5, 1925, a year before Grosser's article was published. At first some thought it might be a prank. But Pompeii had been overrun by an eruption of Mount Vesuvius in A.D. 79. Were there Christians in Pompeii at that time? Yes, Paul had visited near there in A.D. 60 or 61 "where we found brethren [Christians]" (Acts 28:13–14). But there is no proof whatsoever that the Bible or the Lord's Prayer (*paternoster* means "Our Father") existed in the first century in Latin. They were written in Greek, and there is no evidence that the cross was a Christian symbol then (as was the fish). Dr. Thomas R. Forbes, Professor of anatomy and associate dean of the Yale University School of Medicine, writing on this, follows the reasoning of two earlier researches into Sator: "But to reject the theory that the square was invented by or for a Christian seems to leave the alternative that the crosses and paternosters were due to coincidence, which appears impossible."

The crosses and paternosters were "read into" Sator by Christian researchers. My theory is that Sator was a pre-Christian charm, used by worshippers of an older religion, and its discovery at Pompeii is no coincidence. It is well known that many Christian churches have inscribed on them emblems made by "Pagan" craftsmen: the foliate masks of the "Green Men," a disguised Horned God of the Old Religion and the fertility figures called *Shiela-na-gigs* found on many Irish churches. Furthermore, Continental witches, especially the Italian-Sicilian, see in Sator certain secret names which initiated witches are forbidden to divulge.

In the old British town of Cirencester, Gloucestershire, excavators found a piece of painted plaster with the Sator charm inscribed in Roman letters, dating it to the Roman occupation of that town in the third century A.D.

In France, Sator was discovered on a Bible pendant in the Abbey of St. Germain-des-Pres, dating back to A.D. 822; in Egypt on Coptic papyri and on a potsherd; in Germany in a book of amulets published in 1692 at Frankfurt and Leipzig; in Austria on a sixteenth-century coin; in many places in Italy, including the walls, pavements, and columns of churches in Cappadocia and Pieve Tersagni, near Cremona in Asia Minor it was found on a bronze charm dating back to the fourth or fifth century. It was carried to many lands and has been translated into Hebrew, Coptic, Greek, Latin, German, French, and Portuguese, often incorrectly.

The words themselves have been translated to

mean: *sator*, "a sower" or "to sow"; *arepo*, possibly from *arrepo*, "I creep to," and some thought it meant a plow; *tenet*, "to hold," such as a belief; *opera*, "works"; and *rotas*, "wheels." Some of the sentences scholars have ascribed to it are "The sower is at the plow; the labor occupies the wheels" (a fourteenth-century Greek manuscript). "Creative power holds the wheels by a thread" (one researcher said that *arepo* was from *repum*, "thread," and that *arepo* is really two words meaning "a thread"). There is an Ethiopian belief that the five words represent the five wounds of Christ. Another Christian did some word-juggling to come up with: *Pater, oro te, pereat Satan roso*, which means "Father, I pray Thee, let Satan be eaten away." The Jesuit Athanasius Kircher stated in his *Arithmologia* (Kircherus, 1665) that the Sator square was utterly without meaning. One of the greatest researchers into Sator was G. de Jerphanion, whose work was published in French in 1938: *La Voix des Monuments*, at both Rome and Paris, by the Etudes d'Archeologie. He methodically reviews all the arguments, explanations, and ideas offered and does admit that it is possible that the Sator Magic Square could have been "appropriated by Christians."

If Christians insist on "reading into" Sator some of their own beliefs, no harm is done, but followers of the Old Religion can also see in Sator much of their own symbolism: *rotas*, the wheel, is well known in the Craft, the magic Circle. *Opera* can be read as a "working," the witch term for rituals and "work done in the circle." *Tenet* could represent their beliefs, "what I hold to be true." *Sator*, the planting of the seed, whether agrarian or fertility, the chain cycle of life, the belief in Karma and reincarnation, the wheel of life, the Witch *Tenet*: "And ye harm none do as ye will: Do good and it returns to you threefold, do evil and it returns to you threefold"—another way of saying "As ye sow so shall ye reap." And *arepo* is *opera* spelled backwards. All the five words spelled backwards form another word in the square, thus composing palindromes. If it means a plow, it would make sense to worshippers of the Mother Earth Goddess. If it means a thread, that could be a disguise for "rope," also used in certain Witchcraft rites, sometimes to "lay out the circle," other times for the binding of an Initiate. In the word *rotas* can be found both the tora(H) and the taro(T), the former a Jewish sacred book, the latter considered texts of ancient wisdom. There is a belief that the many Jews who lived in Pompeii inscribed Sator on the walls in Latin, inspired by the vision of Ezekiel (Ezekiel 1:16), in which both the words *rota* and *opera* are found in the Vulgate version.

Sator is derived from the same Latin root *satum* from which the God of seed-sowing, Saturn, is derived. The Saturnalia held in his honor on December 17 later became Benevento by Italian witches in that area and then the Witches' Sabbat. The word has now degenerated to mean a sexual orgy.

Arepo could be an abbreviation of Areopagus, a hill west of the Acropolis, Athens, where a high court sat. Also, add an "S" to ARE and you have the Greek God of war Ares (Latin *Mars*), son of Zeus and (H)ERA. He was Aphrodite's lover.

Tenet—doctrine, belief that one "holds."

Opera means not only work but dramas and plays which in ancient times were the means of communicating knowledge and the passing on of the "mysteries." Our modern opera carries on that tradition. Strange that Ops, the Roman Goddess of the harvest, wife of Saturn (Sator), was missed by so many researchers.

Rotas from *rota,* "a wheel." The Roman Catholic Church has a *Sacra Romana Rota* (sacred roman wheel), a court with jurisdiction in ecclesiastical cases (and once in civil ones too); compare with the above-named Areopagus. In modern times we have membership clubs called Rotarians. Note too that *rotas* spelled backwards is *sator,* a form of Saturn, the only planet that has rings around it and attributed with the power to make those influenced by it to "go around in circles."

To my knowledge this may be the first time that in the search for Sator an Old Religionist's point of view has been presented. It could be translated to mean "Saturn holds the plow, works the wheel."

11

Recommended Old Religion Book List

Since there are thousands of books published on "Witchcraft," the sincere and serious student is perplexed. How does one separate the wheat from the chaff? The gold from the mountain of ore? Previously most such books were either written by non-Witches or by authors whose Christian bias was obvious. Then came those books supposedly written by "Witches" which continued the distortion of the Craft of the Wise. Recently, members of the Craft have authored books presenting their own particular views or Craft traditions. Though much more valid than the others, these books do have sectarian prejudice. Yet, like other minorities, Witches do have the right to define themselves. Among the non-Witch authors who are objective and honest are, of course, Margaret Murray's *Witch Cult In Western Europe* and

The God Of The Witches. Old Religionists are fans of the works of poet-author Robert Graves, notably his *White Goddess*, a scholarly, involved, deeply researched and intuitively motivated book. One has to read it in bits and pieces, and then read it again. The classic work of Sir James Frazer, *The Golden Bough*, contains much tradition and folklore.

Charles Godfrey Leland of course is required reading. Among his many books that have been recently reprinted are *Aradia, Or Gospel of The Witches, Etruscan Magic and Occult Remedies, Gypsy Sorcery and Fortune Telling*, and *The Mystic Will*. The latter was originally published in London in 1899 under the title *Have You A Strong Will?* Later it was republished in the United States in 1911 by the Yogi Publication Company. Then it was forgotten until republished in 1972 by this author's Hero Press. All of the above are recommended by WICA, together with the following: *Witches: Investigating An Ancient Religion* by T. C. Lethbridge (one of the best), *Witchcraft: The Sixth Sense* by Justine Glass, *Where Witchcraft Lives* by Doreen Valiente, and *The Witches Speak* by Patricia Crowther. These last two are Initiated Witch High Priestesses in England.

Gerald B. Gardner's books, *The Meaning of Witchcraft* and *Witchcraft Today*, provide a good insight into that branch of the Craft named after him. Two books on Alexandrian Witchcraft, the sect founded by Alex Sanders in England, are *King of the Witches* by June Johns and *What Witches Do* by Stewart Farrar. The first is a rather sensationalized biography of Sanders. It includes their "Book Of Shadows," which is very similar to the Gardnerian's. In America there is *Lady Sheba's Book Of Shadows*, which was incorporated into her larger book, *The Grimoire of Lady Sheba*. A comparison of her *Shadows* and the one published in *King Of The Witches* shows they are almost identical. Since I've also seen and recopied the Gardnerian *Book of Shadows*, I was in a position to compare them page by page. Lady Sheba did rearrange some of the rites, notably her version of Drawing Down The Moon and her misnaming some of the Sabbats. However, for the newcomer to the Craft, it's a good basic sourcebook. If and or when Initiated, the student will have his own book anyway.

Another book that gives basics is *Mastering Witchcraft* by Paul Huson. Conservative Crafters were dismayed by some of the things he wrote, yet the book has a fund of knowledge for the student. He will learn correct Craft theology once admitted to a Witch training group (if he's fortunate enough to find one). *Psychic Self Defense* by Dion Fortune, one of the early members of the Golden Dawn and Founder of the Society of Inner Light, a practising occultist and lay psychoanalyst, offers self-protection methods against what is termed "psychic attack."

Once you've been initiated into Old Religion theology you can read the following books which are spotty craftwise but do contain some good information: *Witchcraft* by Pennethorne Hughes, *Witchcraft, Magic, and Occultism* by W. B. Crow, and *The Truth About Witchcraft* by Hans Holzer. Another one of Holzer's books is *The New Pagans*, which raised a storm of controversy in some of the Pagan publications. A large portion of it is devoted to Fred Adams, founder and theoretician of Feraferia, whose publication is *Korythalia*. Tim Zell, founder of the Church of All Worlds and editor of their letter-packed *Green Egg*, who was also one of the founding members of Council of Themis, was given only passing mention. Eventually, because of various conflicts, many of the members of Council of Themis broke away and formed a new group called Council of Earth Religions.

A paperback called *Witches, U.S.A.* by Susan Roberts is supposedly an "inside" treatment of the subject in which the author was invited by certain Witches themselves into their homes and confidence. It centers primarily on an insular, chauvinist, and book-based group of Witches who really fancied themselves as the "Keepers of the Holy Grail." Most of them are underground—what I call still in their "broomclosets"—and their yardstick of "genuineness" is based on nothing more than their like or dislike of certain individuals. Despite all their pretensions they basically lack integrity and play a game of "If you recognize me as a Witch I'll recognize you as one." Their "recognition" is of course utterly valueless. They have a right to be discreet, but that's not a synonym for dishonesty. This book is highly praised by them since it presents the "image" they desire. Whether the author was completely taken in or withheld some of the truth under the guise of "confidence," I don't know. Anyway, I met the author before she completed her book. I was deliberately not mentioned. This same group publishes an insignificant "Craft paper" in which they've recommended groups and publications that have nothing to do with the Craft but prejudicially never mentioned my own. They highly recommended a certain outfit in Long Island which was a "front" for a well-known Gardnerian. This same outfit was blasted by David Techter in his Books column in the December, 1972, *Fate* magazine. These people ignorantly thought that they were really in, but were completely in the dark about Witch covens that have existed in America since the eighteenth century. They not only do not have any contact with these covens, but the latter absolutely refuse to have anything to do with them. They may or may not be valid as Witches, but as people they have no value to us. During the composition of this book one of the Witches was killed in a shooting accident. His friend was later killed in a car crash (frontpaged in *WICA Newsletter*). I might add that not one of these "Witches" sent one word of encouragement when I had my civil rights battles with New York's Parks Department. However, their chief spokesman, who hides behind a pseudonym did attend our Witch-In as a "spy," and we have him on film. Later he was invited to a small gathering at my apartment. He thought it was a heaven-sent opportunity to spy on me, little realizing that I knew who he was all along. I wanted to see how he operated and taperecorded the conversation that evening. In psychology it's well-known that hostility towards someone is often a defense against guilt, and he and his cohorts were guilty. They've done absolutely nothing to implement religious freedom or civil rights for Witches. Even simple logic should have told him that I, like most people, simply don't invite complete strangers into my home.

My own book *Black Magic, Satanism, and Voodoo* is not a how-to book, but challenges certain individuals and groups in the Craft who reveal Judeo-Christian hangups and others who make outrageous claims. Besides "The War Of The Witches," there's a chapter on homosexuality and an interview with Anton Szandor LaVey of the Church of Satan. *Curses In Verses* is the Old Religion in rhymed prose (I'm not a poet and wouldn't dare presume to call it poetry). The one entitled "Roman Robin Hoods" reveals much about my Sicilian *strege* ancestors. *Weird Ways Of Witchcraft* was written more as a reporter than as a Witch (I hadn't gone public yet) with the emphasis on "Weird," that portion of the Craft which has been generally assumed by the public. "The Witch Manifesto" and the chapter on "The Curse On The Catholic Church" made some of the broomcloset Witches run for cover. As I've said before, for my part they can all go back underground—preferably six feet of it.

Aidan Kelly, founder of the New, Reformed, Orthodox Order of the Golden Dawn, and publisher of *Witches Trine* magazine, recently wrote me, "I find much in Paul Huson's *Mastering Witchcraft* that could be very harmful to beginners, because it is such a mixed bag, and because he says *nothing* about Karma or Craft Laws. I find it a very useful sourcebook in certain areas, but only because I already knew how to sort it out. If I were teaching a class, and had to use just *one* textbook, I'd use Stewart Farrar's *What Witches Do* at this point—until my own finally gets published."

For those interested in the Welsh tradition, *The Mabinogion*, translated by Lady Charlotte Guest, is required reading. A good book for Celtic tradition (of which Welsh is one branch) is *The Religion of the Ancient Celts* by J. A. MacCulloch. Many of these books are now out of print and may be obtained only from antiquarian bookdealers. Some are expensive, but worth it. In this vein the following books all contain valuable information: *Observations on the Popular Antiquities of Great Britain* by the Reverend J. Brand (3 volumes, 1870); *Popular Tales of the West Highlands* by J. F. Campbell (4 volumes, Edinburgh, 1890); *Super-

stitions of the Highlands and Islands of Scotland and *Witchcraft and Second Sight in the Highlands and Islands of Scotland* by J. G. Campbell (1900 and 1902); *Tales of the Fairies and Ghost World* by J. Curtin (1895); *The Cuchullin Saga* by E. Hull (London, 1898); *Old Celtic Romances* by P. W. Joyce (London, 1894); *Legendary Fictions of the Irish Celts* by P. Kennedy (1894); *Folk-Lore of the Isle of Man* by A. W. Moore (1891); *The Voyage of Bran* by A. Nutt and K. Meyer (2 volumes, 1895–1897); *Manners and Customs of the Ancient Irish* by E. O'Curry (4 volumes, London, 1873); *The Arthurian Legend* (1891), *Celtic Britain* (1908), *Celtic Folk-lore* (2 volumes, 1901) all by Sir John Rhys, published in London. And the rare but invaluable *Four Ancient Books of Wales* by W. F. Skene, published in Edinburgh, 1868, in two volumes.

A book that lists various "rites, ceremonies, observances, and miscellaneous antiquities" alphabetically is *Curiosities of Popular Customs* by William S. Walsh, first published in Philadelphia, 1897. *The Book of Days*, edited by R. Chambers, was published in two volumes in London in 1883. It lists all the various feast days and "popular antiquities" by date. Two books by Lewis Spence which have much Craft folklore are *Legends and Romances of Brittany* and *Mysteries of Britain*. Some of the newer popular books are my own *Witches' Liberation and Practical Guide to Covens, Sex and the Single Psychic*, and *1000 Witchcraft Questions Answered*. My *Understanding the Tarot* is an updated, streamlined book on tarot divination that touches on the Old Religion. *Witchcraft From The Inside* and *Witchcraft: Ancient and Modern* by Raymond Buckland present the Gardnerian viewpoint as well as his own. *Witch Blood: The Diary Of A Witch High*

Priestess by Patricia Crowther, is mostly an autobiographical work detailing her friendship with Gerald Gardner, her Witch wedding to her husband Arnold, a professional stage conjurist, her subsequent Initiation into the Craft, and her meeting with Aleister Crowley. An excellent book of Old Religion poetry written by a Witch High Priest who has been nearly blind since birth is *Thorns of the Blood Rose* by Victor H. Anderson. Vance Randolph's *Ozark Magick and Folklore* presents that part of Americana that retains the remnants of the Old Religion in its various rites, rituals, and folklore, but that has forgotten its theological heritage.

Witches and ceremonial magicians both employ Magick, but their approaches and aims are usually quite different, though there are overlappings. The following books deal not with the Old Religion but with Magick, and should be read with that understanding. *Magic, Its Ritual Power and Purpose* and *The Magician: His Training and Work* are both by W. E. Butler. Two books by Francis King containing personality profiles, occult gossip, and ritual magick rites are *Ritual Magick In England*, published in the United States as *The Rites Of Modern Occult Magic*, and his newest, *Sexuality, Magic and Perversion*. Louis T. Culling's two books *The Complete Magickal Curriculum of the Secret Order G. B. G.* and *A Manual of Sex Magick* are recommended by modern ceremonial Magicians. Many of these books are very involved, and some of them utterly useless to practitioners of the Old Religion who prefer the simple unpretentious rites of their own faith to the highly complex rites of ceremonial magicians. Students of the subject advise that these books should only be read by those who are advanced. Franz Bardon's *Initiation into Hermetics, The Practice of Magical Evocation*, and

The Key to the True Quabbalah are considered classics, Aleister Crowley's works contain many pitfalls and booby-traps; the inexperienced are cautioned about trying to employ some of the methods, though his *Magick in Theory and Practice* is still avidly read. The four-volume *The Golden Dawn* by Israel Regardie has recently been republished in two large volumes. He once was the secretary to Aleister Crowley, with whom he performed many of the rituals and ceremonies. His other books, *The Middle Pillar, The Tree of Life,* and *A Garden of Pomegranates,* all contain much ritual and information for the interested student. A classic in this field is *The Sacred Magick of Abramelin The Mage,* translated by MacGregor Mathers, once head of the Golden Dawn, and with whom Aleister Crowley had a magickal feud. Most Witches find the various Christian-written *Grimoires* just so much gibberish though the *Key of Solomon* does contain some useful information. Indries Shaw's *The Secret Lore Of Magic* contains four such works, including the *Grimoire of Honorius The Great* and *Secrets of Albertus Magnus.*

Neo-Paganism is much more liberal than the various Witchcraft groups with their oaths of secrecy and sectarian views. It can also be a steppingstone to an Old Religion coven for those willing to put in the time and work, getting their training in the many Pagan groves in the United States and abroad. Others simply prefer the new Paganism. These include Fred Adam's *Feraferia,* devoted to the worship of the pre-Christian Mother Goddess, Harold Moss's *Church of the Eternal Source,* a recreation of authentic Egyptian religion, the various groups who make up the membership in the *Council of Themis* and the *Council of Earth Religions,* and the *Church of All Worlds,* headed by Tim

Zell, a pioneer in this field, whose publication *Green Egg* is an open forum for all these various traditions, including Witches.

Among some of the books listed in the Church of All Worlds Bibliography for "Pagan Religion" are *The Golden Bough* by Sir James Frazer, *Man and His Symbols* by Carl Gustav Jung, and *The White Goddess* by Robert Graves. Feraferian philosophy, which delves into the Eleusinian mysteries, also recommends the latter, and W. Holman Keith recommends that one read *Man Into Wolf: An Anthropological Interpretation of Sadism, Masochism, and Lycanthropy*. Michael E. Hurley, who reviews books for *Green Egg*, recommends the following: *The Religions of Man*, Huston Smith; *Man Seeks The Divine*, A. E. Bury; *The Religious Experience of Mankind*, Ninian Smith; *The Perennial Philosophy*, Aldous Huxley; *Religious and Spiritual Groups In Modern America*, Robert Ellwood; *The New Religions*, Jacob Needleman; and *Gurus, Swarmis, and Avatars*, M. H. Harper; *Stranger In A Strange Land*, Robert Heinlein; *Anthem*, Ayn Rand; and *The Prophet*, Kahlil Gibran.

This list is merely a guide and undoubtedly has omitted many other good books on the Old Religion, Paganism, and even Magick. However, it is a springboard for your own study and researches. If you find yourself responding both intellectually and emotionally when reading the recommended books, then you will know that either the Old Religion or Paganism is for you.

12

Questions and Answers

Q. What are the major feast-days of Witches? Could you tell me more about the origins of Halloween?

A. Most Anglo-American covens celebrate the following holy days. The four major ones are Olmelc or Candlemas on February 2; May Eve, Beltane, or Walpurgisnacht on April 30; Lammas on July 31 or August 1; and of course Halloween or Samhain on October

31. The four minor Holy Days are the two solstices: Yule, around December 22; and Midsummer, around June 21 and 22. The other two are the equinoxes: March 20–21 for spring and the fall equinox on September 22 or 23.

The following will help to give you some idea of the origins of Halloween:

November Eve, All Hallows' Eve, the Gaelic fire festival of Samhain, now generally called Halloween, represents the summer's end, when the Earth Goddess turns over her reign to the Horned God of the Hunt, the transition from life to death, from an agrarian time to one of hunting, from summer to winter, from warmth to coldness, from light to darkness. It has been Christianized into All Saints' Day, a time when the souls of the departed wander the land and in some cases where the souls of the living temporarily join their spirit brethren, a time for mediumship, remembrance of departed loved ones, and celebration (as opposed to mourning) of the dead.

The Roman Goddess of fruits and seeds, Pomona, was worshipped on this day. The stored fruits and seeds of the summer were then opened for the celebrants. Apples and nuts were the main fruits. This was also the autumn harvest festival of the Druids. They believed in the transmigration of souls and taught that Saman, the Lord of Death, summoned those wicked souls who were condemned to occupy the bodies of animals in the preceding twelve months. The accused believed that they could propitiate Saman by gifts and incantations, thus lessening if not eliminating their sentences. This was also the time when the Druids lit huge bonfires in honor of Baal, a custom continued in Britain and Wales until recent times.

In Ireland October 31 was called *Oidhche Shamhna,* or Vigil of Saman. In his *Collectanea de Rebus Hibernicis,* Villancey says that in Ireland the peasants assembled with clubs and sticks, "going from house to house, collecting money, breadcake, butter, cheese, eggs, etc., for the feast, repeating verses in honor of the solemnity, demanding preparations for the festival in the name of St. Columb Kill, desiring them to lay aside the fatted calf and to bring forth the black sheep. The good women are employed in making the griddle-cake and candles; these last are sent from house to house in the vicinity, and are lighted up on the (Saman) next day, before which they pray, or are supposed to pray, for the departed soul of the donor. Every house abounds in the best viands they can afford: apples and nuts are devoured in abundance; the nutshells are burnt, and from the ashes many strange things are foretold; cabbages are torn up by the root; hemp-seed is sown by the maidens, and they believe that if they look back they will see the apparition of the man intended for their future spouse; they hang a smock before the fire, on the close of the feast, and sit up all night, concealed in a corner of the room, convinced that his apparition will come down the chimney and turn the smock; they throw a ball of yarn out of the window, and wind it on the reel within, convinced that if they repeat the Pater Noster backwards, and look at the ball of yarn without, they will then also see his sith or apparition; they dip for apples in a tub of water, and endeavor to bring one up in the mouth; they suspend a cord with a cross-stick, with apples at one point, and candles lighted at the other, and endeavor to catch the apple, while it is in a circular motion, in the mouth."

Vallancey concludes that these practices are the remnants of Druidism and will never be eradicated while the name of Saman remains. In this brief passage we see the origins of many modern Halloween practices, such as trick or treat, the Jack-o-Lantern, and apple bobbing.

In the island of Lewis the name Shamhna, or Saman, was called Shony. One writer in disgust described "an ancient custom here to sacrifice to a sea-god, called Shony, at Hallowtide." Curiosities of Popular Customs, William S. Walsh, J. B. Lippincott, Philadelphia, 1907. The supposed Christian inhabitants would gather at the Church of St. Mulvay, each family bringing provisions and malt which was brewed into ale. They chose one of themselves to wander into the sea at night up to his waist. He then poured out a cup of ale calling upon Shony to bless his people for the coming year. "At his return," this writer says, "they all went to church, where there was a candle burning upon the altar: and then standing silent for a little time, one of them gave a signal, at which the candle was put out, and immediately all of them went to the fields, where they fell a-drinking their ale, and spent the remainder of the night in dancing and singing. The ministers in Lewis told me they spent several years before they could persuade the vulgar natives to abandon this ridiculous piece of superstition."

The name *Saman* shows evidence of Druidism in the Irish. Another word, the name of a drink, is "lambswool." It is made from bruising roasted apples and mixing it with ale or milk. The *Gentlemen's Magazine* for May, 1784, says, "this is a constant ingredient at a merrymaking on Holy Eve." Vallancey shrewdly traced its etymological origin when he said, "The first day of November was dedicated to the angel presiding over fruits, seeds, etc., and was therefore named *La Mas Ubhal,*—that is, the day of the apple fruit,—and being pronounced Lamasool, the English have corrupted the name to Lambs-wool." The "angel" referred to of course is the Roman Goddess Pomona.

The black American expressions of "having soul" and the popularity of their "soul food," which at one time was the leftovers from the slavemaster's tables, have their counterpart in old Halloween pastries, made on All Souls' Day or All Hallows' Eve. An old saying goes, "A Soule Cake, a Soule-cake, have mercy on all Christen soules for a Soule-cake." In a book called *The Festyvall,* published in 1511, a custom is mentioned which was obsolete even then: "We rede," it says, "in olde tyme good people wolde on All halowen daye bake brade and dele it for all crysten soules." In Thomas Tusser's *Five Hundred Points of Good Husbandry* (1580), he writes:

Wife, some time this weeke, if the wether hold cleere,
And end of wheat-sowing we make for this yeare,
Remember you, therefore, though I do it not,
The Seed-Cake, the Pasties, and Furmentie pot.

Tollet, in a note in his *Variorum Shakespeare* to the "Two Gentlemen of Verona" (II, 2) says, "It is worth remarking that on All Saint's Day the poor people in Staffordshire, and perhaps on other country places, go from parish to parish *a-soul-ing,* as they call it, i.e., begging and puling [or singing small, as *Bailey's Dictionary* explains *puling*] for Soul Cakes, or any good thing to make them merry. This custom is mentioned by Peck, and seems a remnant of Popish superstition to pray for departed souls, particularly those of friends."

What Tollet attributes to "Popish superstitions" of course is the Church's incorporation of the feast of Pomona. Under the Christian cloak is concealed an ancient pagan festival of the dead, as Frazer has said in his *Golden Bough*. It was considered the beginning of winter and in many places the date when the New Year began. In the Isle of Man "Manx mummers used to go around on Hallowe'en (Old Style) singing, in the Manx language, a sort of Hogmanay song which began, 'Tonight is New Year's Night, Hogunnaa!' In Ireland, a new fire used to be kindled every year on Hallowe'en or the Eve of Samhain, and from this sacred flame all the fires of Ireland were rekindled. Such a custom points strongly to Samhain or All Saints' Day (the first of November) as New Year's Day; since the annual kindling of a new fire takes place most naturally at the beginning of the year, in order that the blessed influence of the fresh fire may last throughout the whole period of twelve months." Frazer also points out that this was the time when the ancient Celts resorted to all kinds of divination in order to know their fortunes for the coming year.

Q. Are these Holy Days the same throughout the world?

A. No. However, there are many universal similarities between all the pagan religions. Names, dates, and days vary according to national origin. For instance, one of the Holy Days still celebrated by many Italian and some Sicilian traditions is the *Lupercalia*, on February 15. It has since been Christianized into St. Valentine's Day on Feb. 14. Let me quote from the

WICA Newsletter: Ancient Roman festival honoring Lupercus, God of Fertility. It was called *dies februatus* meaning 'day of expiation.' The Lupercal—'wolf's grotto'—a cave on the western slope of Palatine Hill. Near it was the *ficus ruminalis,* the fig tree under which Romulus and Remus were found and nursed by a she-wolf. The Lupercai who celebrated this yearly festival were made up of the Fabian who belonged to the Sabines and the Quintilian Lupercai, the Latins. Later in honor to Julius Caesar, there was added the Julian Brotherhood. They sacrificed a goat. Young neophytes, usually two, were brought in. The High Priest touched their foreheads with the bloody knife. Then another priest wiped away the blood with wool dipped into milk. The feast began with the celebrants clothed only in goat skins and carrying (really hiding) thongs made from the same goat hides. They ran up and down the streets of the city striking anyone who passed them. Women came forward to be hit by the goat-thongs, believing it enhanced their own fertility. This was also a symbolic purification of the land and of the persons touched. This was one of the last Pagan rites to be given up before Christianity completely dominated the country. It is still celebrated today but in modified form, without the goat or any other kind of sacrifice, but all wearing skins and goat horns in a special *strege* ritual."

Q. Have there been any books published that give the true poetic feeling of the Old Religion?

A. Yes. One of the best is *Thorns of the Blood Rose* by Victor H. Anderson, nearly blind since birth, yet a High Priest of the Old Religion. The book contains much of Craft lore and symbolism and has been highly praised by members of nearly all Witch traditions. The following poem from this book will give you an idea of his poetic power:

The Temple Of Words

Could we have met as pagan children meet,
   Could we have loved as pagan children love,
Caressing Mother Earth with naked feet,
   Raising our eyes and outspread hands above
To revel in the purity of blue,
   I might have told with warm simplicity,
The one, clear, shining truth of love to you,
   Beyond the kiss, in rhythmic ecstasy.
But I must build a temple of my words
   (Her many breasted statue of white stone)
While all my passions like a swarm of birds
   Sing in the sunlight as I pray alone.
One word ill-placed and down the structure falls,
Crushing a broken dream between the walls.

Q. What are some of the Christian holy days that are based upon or borrowed from ancient Pagan Religions?

A. You'll find many of them discussed in this book. However, briefly, here are some of them: December 25 in ancient times was the day celebrated in honor of the sun, deified in such figures as Mithra, Osiris, Horus, and Adonis. It was also the feast day of Bacchus, Krishna, Sakia, and others. The legends of these Gods were the same as those attributed to Jesus Christ by the early Church. Pope Julius I in A.D. 337 made December 25 the official day to celebrate Jesus's birth, following older traditions who honored their founders on that date. It was also the ancient celebration of the winter solstice. There is absolutely no record in the Bible or elsewhere of when Jesus Christ was born.

All of us are still paying tribute to the ancient Gods and Goddesses by the names of our days of the week.

English	French	Italian	Spanish	Planet	GOD
Sunday	Dimanche	Domani	Domingo	Sun	Mithra
Monday	Lundi	Lunedi	Lunes	Moon	Diana
Tuesday	Mardi	Martedi	Martes	Mars	Tiw
Wednesday	Mercredi	Mercoledi	Miercoles	Mercury	Mercury
Thursday	Jeudi	Giovedi	Jueves	Jupiter	Jove—Thor
Friday	Vendredi	Venerdi	Viernes	Venus	Venus—Freya
Saturday	Samedi	Sabato	Sabado	Saturn	Saturn

Two of the English names come from Old Saxon rather than Latin. Tiw's Day became Tuesday in honor of the old Teutonic deity, Tiw or Tives. Wednesday is named after the old Teutonic Norse God Wodan or Wotan. The Saxon word for day is *doeg*. In olden times the days were called Jove's Doeg (Thursday), Mercury's Doeg (Wednesday), Mar's Doef (Tuesday), etc. Friday was the day when the ancients paid tribute to Venus—the love day. When Christianity became dominant, Friday was no longer considered lucky—Jesus was crucified on that day; also, the uninhibited sexual rites dedicated to the love Goddess Venus was considered a great "sin." Besides the days of our week our months are also named after ancient deities:

January: From Latin *Januarius*, honoring Janus, a Roman God. He presided over the Gates of Heaven, which the Christians later assigned to St. Peter. The Anglo-Saxons called it *Aefter-Yule*, and prior to that *Wolf-monat*.

February: From *Februus*, another name for the God of purification Faunus, thus fertility. The feast was held on February 15 (see Lupercalia) and was called *Februa*.

March: After Mars, God of War. Anglo-Saxons called it *Hraed-monat,* rugged month, or *Hlyd-monat,* stormy month. A stormy March was an omen of poor crops. A dry March indicated a rich harvest.

April: From Latin *aperio* "to open," like buds. Anglo-Saxons called it *Easter-monat,* in honor of the Teutonic Goddess of the same name. She ruled spring and light. The Romans dedicated this month to Venus, often referring to it as *Mensis Veneris* instead of *Aprilis.*

May: Named after *Maia Majesta,* ancient Roman Goddess of Spring. Considered Vulcan's wife. Look up the folklore regarding the May Day celebrations, bonfires, and other rites celebrated throughout Europe.

June: Named after Roman Goddess Juno. Called *Sear-monat* by Anglo-Saxons. Juno was Queen of Heaven and Guardian of Marriage and ruled childbirth. June is still the most favored month for marriage today.

July: Originally called *Quintilus,* the fifth month. Old Saxons called it *Maed-monat*—"mead month"—the time to gather honey for the drink called mead.

August: Named after the Roman Emperor Augustus. Was once called *Sixtilis,* the sixth month.

September: Named after the Latin number for seven, that being that month in the old calender. Saxons called it *Gerst-monat,* barley month, as this crop was usually gathered then.

October: From *octo,* the eighth month in old calendar. Saxons named it *Wyn-monat,* "wine month." This was harvest time, and Bacchhus and Dionysius and all the other ancient deities were honored. See Halloween above.

November: From the ninth month in old Roman calendar. Saxons called it ·*Blot-monat,* "blood month."

This was when the cattle and sheep were slaughtered for food and sacrifices.

December: Named after tenth month in old calendar. It was consecrated to Saturn, and on December 17 the great feast of *Saturnalia* began, lasting several days. It coincided with the winter solstice and the Yule season, which Christianity turned into their Christmas–New Year celebrations. The Anglo-Saxons called it *Yule-monat,* "midwinter-month." The word *Yule* comes from Icelandic *Hjol,* "wheel," the complete turn of the seasonal cycle, and the wheel of course is an ancient solar and life symbol. The zodiac, of course, is a wheel.

Q. Why did you choose the Craft name of Nemesis? Doesn't this indicate a vengeful streak?

A. No. I chose it because it's the name of the Greek Goddess of retributive justice. All Witches claim to believe in Karma, and one of their tenets is "Do good and it will return to you threefold. Do evil and it will return to you threefold." Karma makes no allowances for mercy or pity or revenge or stupidity. Bad judgment breeds bad results. Simply put, "What's good for you is good for me." Those who insist on calling this revenge are trying to sidestep Karmic consequences. It's an attempt to blackmail you psychically so that you do not claim your rights and permit them to get away with imposition, parasiticism, and evil. Those who hate the concept of justice (and by the way my sign is Libra, the scales of justice), will be the first to use the words *revenge* or *vengeful.* I give no one the right to do me wrong. I despise people who whitewash wrongdoing and blackball those who have integrity. Under no circumstances will I permit anyone to think that they can get away with it and I most certainly will never be a consenting victim. As to compromise: What is the result of "compromising" black paint with white paint? Or dropping some ink into a pitcher of clear water? Why is it that it's always those who have done you wrong who talk about mercy, forgiveness, and compromise? And who use the words *revenge* and *unspiritual* as a psychic blackmailing weapon on those who lack self-esteem and a clearcut sense of right and wrong? These people are not worth cultivating. Reject them. No matter what label they use—"good Christians," "white witches," "altruists"—they are basically psychic vampires, spiritual leeches, emotional bloodsuckers. They hate the concept of justice because it represents the true law of Karma, practised by true Witches, which permits no room for those who pursue evil under the guise of a misunderstood idea of what Witchcraft is. These are the same people who worry about being under psychic attack. They should. The demons of their own guilt will give them no peace. Vengeful themselves, they expect the same. What they don't realize is that the best revenge stems from justice. Their own thoughts and lives are hate-filled and unfulfilled. This is why I've said repeatedly: "The worst curse that I can wish on anyone is—HIMSELF." See my book *How To Prevent Psychic Blackmail* for more on this subject.

Q. Is it true that Witches are forbidden to accept money for their services?

A. Yes and no. No Witch will charge a fee for any kind of work done in the circle, for healing, for Magick. Unlike ministers of major religions, though, the Witch is self-supporting. She or he is not paid a salary. There are no collection plates or donations, and most of them have not registered as a religion with the city or state simply because they prefer to remain incognito, to worship quietly, and live their own lives in their own way. However, if a Witch renders an honest service, writes a book, gives a lecture, or makes genuine Craft artifacts for others she or he is entitled to a just compensation, especially when you realize that those who have made the most money on Witchcraft (whether pro or con or spurious) have been non-Witches. If an Initiated Witch runs a bookstore or Craft supply shop, the items aren't gotten free. The rent must be paid. Tangible items (books, records, jewelry, candles, incense, athames) are entitled to tangible compensation. Intangible services such as healing and Magick done volitionally by members of a coven, are not entitled to tangible compensation. The reward here comes from the positive results to the recipient. Material goods should be exchanged for other material goods (usually money). Spiritual goods are exchanged for spiritual compensation.

Since I'm well known, I often get letters of woe asking for help and advice. When these people are genuinely in need I place their names on the healing lists with the various covens with which I meet. I tell them I will and write, "There are three things that I cannot give you: time, personal attention, and faith." Those idiots who request that I hex someone, adding, "I'm willing to pay good money," have their letters thrown into the garbage can. Many of these people are parasites. They impose on you by writing an eight-to twenty-page letter and don't even have the decency to enclose a stamp for reply. Those who are sincerely in need will be helped by the coven healings. As to the others, they eliminate themselves. What they want is personal attention at my expense, usually in the form of a "reading," and of course operating on the supposition that their need is a claim on your thoughts, your time, and your talents. Most of them don't give a damn about the Old Religion. A Witch is merely someone that they can use to serve their own ends—a psychic sucker—and when rebuffed, off they go seeking a new victim. Thank the Goddess that I am a professional handwriting analyst. One glance tells me all I need to know and I act accordingly.

An unbelievable number of high schools, colleges and Universities write to me asking for "free sample copies" of the *WICA Newsletter*. I tell them, "when my printer is willing to give me free samples of his work I'll gladly send you free samples of our Newsletter. Since your school has funds and all of you are paid a salary—which is not true of Witch High Priests and Witch High Priestesses—it will be less of a burden for you to subscribe than for us to deplete our own supply by sending out free samples."

Ditto all those "students" who are writing "theme papers on Witchcraft," expecting me to supply them with all of their research material free. I usually send them the Recommended Book List and let them take it from there. Others are looking for pen pals and would be "honored if I correspond with them." Then there are a few really obnoxious individuals who write to every known Witch, compare answers, quote one Witch to another, and in this way try to obtain information and "secrets." They usually manage to get one or two courteous letters and that's it. They become *persona non grata*.

If a Witch is a professionally trained person in the fields of counseling, psychology, graphology, parapsychology, or astrology, she or he has a right to charge for professional services like anyone else. No one has the right to ask another to work for nothing. These other abilities may be vocations or avocations entitled to compensation. Witchcraft itself is a religion (when genuinely practiced and not used as a lure for clients). A psychic Witch must be constantly on guard so that parasitic people don't drain his or her energies. If I didn't have an unlisted phone number I could be on the phone twenty-four hours a day. As it is, there are people who call the phone company making up all kinds of wild excuses and lies, including one they told me about. A woman in Palm Beach, Florida, insisted that she was dying, that I was her personal physician, and only I could save her. I told the official, "The only people who have my number are those I care about. As for the others—let them die!" This may sound harsh, but it's the only way to treat people who intend to impose. As I've said before, "The only way to treat a psychic vampire is to stick a verbal stake through its heart."

Q. What are the Witch greetings?

A. "Blessed Be" and "Merry meet. Merry part."

Q. Are there any statues of the Pagan Gods and Goddesses in public buildings in America?

A. I haven't researched this. However, the old Madison Square Garden on Madison Square New York City, which was demolished in 1924 for a newer one, had a tower which contained a 13-foot copper statue of Diana, Goddess of the Hunt, sculptured by St. Gaudens. It towered 332 feet above the street. When it came down many private individuals wanted it, including certain millionaires, but Diana was finally given to the Philadelphia Museum of Art and is still there at the head of the Great Stair Hall.

Q. Who has the largest collection of books on Witchcraft, sorcery, demonology, and the occult?

A. The Vatican Library in Rome. In America the Andrew Dickson White library at Cornell University has one of the largest collections of material relating to witchcraft—or at least what has been described as such—in the world. Both White and his pupil George Lincoln Burr (1857–1938) were scholars and researchers into this subject.

Q. Though Witchcraft claims that the woman holds the most important role as the representative of the Goddess on earth, it's the male Witches who have been the most dominant. Isn't this a contradiction?

A. No. The Craft permits each individual to function in the areas in which he or she is most qualified. Many women in the Craft are underground. They prefer to devote their time and energies to their roles of High Priestess. Those who have the talent and the interest to lecture, write books, give interviews, are free to do so. The women are dominant *in the Craft* but not necessarily in public relations. True, in some cases this may reflect the general patriarchal trend of all society, wherein the male has been the outspoken one on matters of theology, philosophy, and religion. If few Wicca women speak with authority to the media on the Craft it's because they haven't made themselves known. Those traditions which insist on remaining incognito can't complain. Others, who are open or have "gone public," have the same opportunity as the male Witches to make themselves heard. If more male Witches write on the subject than the female ones, who's to blame for that? The female "Witches" who do get media attention are often self-designated and fit the stereotypes wanted. Again, it's a question of ability, desire, qualification, and personal initiative. Since it's still a male chauvinist society, the Male Witch can often confront patriarchal males on their own ground. When one little Craft publication insisted that Witches had no need for Women's Liberation, in an article written by a supposed male Witch, the female Witches were silent. Of course this person expressed only his own views. I challenged him on this in the *WICA Newsletter*. Again I repeat: *The female Witch is dominant in the Craft.* Outside the Craft, especially where the media is concerned, it has been the male Witch who has been heard. Qualified Old Religion High Priestesses can rectify this matter. But that's a personal matter, a private choice, for each one to make.

Q. What can members of the Old Religion and of the Witches Anti-Defamation League do when they read articles which discriminate?

A. You can send letters of protest and explanation to the offending publication. The following letters of mine will serve as examples. Most have not been published, but "Nothing ventured, nothing gained."

Bibliography

Adams, E. H. Davenport, *Witch, Warlock, and Magician,* Chatto and Windus, London, 1889

Ahmed, Rollo, *The Black Arts,* Paperback Library, New York, 1968

Anderson, Victor H., *Thorns of the Blood Rose,* Cora Anderson, San Leandro, California, 1970

Bach, Marcus, *Strange Altars,* Signet Mystic Books, New York, 1968

Bonomo, Giuseppe, *Caccia alle Streghe: La credenza nelle streghe dal secolo Xiii al six con Particolare Riferimento all'Italia,* Palermo, Sicily, 1959

Bracelin, Jack L., *Gerald Gardner: Witch,* Octogon Press, London, n.d.

Buckland, Raymond, *Witchcraft: Ancient and Modern,* H-C Publishers, New York, 1970

————, *Witchcraft from the Inside,* Llewellyn Publications, St. Paul, Minnesota, 1971

Cabot, Tracy, *Inside the Cults,* Holloway House, Los Angeles, 1970

Caron, M., and Hutchin, S., *The Alchemists,* Grove Press, New York, 1961

Castaneda, Carlos, *Teachings of Don Juan: A Yaqui Way of Knowledge,* Ballantine Books, New York, 1969

Crow, W. B., *Witchcraft, Magic, and Occultism,* Wilshire Book Company, Los Angeles, 1972

Crowley, Aleister, *The Confessions of Aleister Crowley,* Bantam Books, New York, 1971

Crowther, Patricia, *The Witches Speak,* Athol Publishers, Isle Of Man, 1965

————, *Witch Blood,* H-C Publishers, New York, 1973

Daraul, Arkon, *History of Secret Societies,* Citadel Press, New York, 1962

Dingwell, Eric J., and Langdon-Davies, John, *The Unknown: Is It Never?*, Signet Books, New York, 1956

Dumas, Francois R., *Cagliostro*, Orion Press, New York, 1967

Ebon, Martin, ed., *Witchcraft Today*, Signet Mystic Books, New York, 1970

Elworthy, Frederick Thomas, *Horns of Honour*, John Murray, London, 1900

———, *The Evil Eye*, John Murray, London, 1895

Farrar, Stewart, *What Witches Do*, Coward, McCann, and Geoghegan, New York, 1971

Frazer, Sir James G., *The Golden Bough*, Macmillan Company, New York, 1958

Fort, Charles, *The Book of the Damned*, Boni and Liveright, New York, 1919

Fortune, Dion, *Psychic Self-Defense*, Sam Weiser, New York, 1971

Gardner, Gerald B., *Witchcraft Today*, Citadel Press, New York, 1955

———, *Meaning of Witchcraft*, Aquarian Press, London, 1959

Garrett, Eileen J., *Sense and Nonsense of Prophecy*, Creative Age Press, New York, 1950

Ginsburg, Carlo, I., *Benandanti: Ricerche sulle Stregoneria e sui Culti Agrari, etc.*, Turin, Italy, 1966

Glass, Justine, *Witchcraft: The Sixth Sense*, Neville Spearman, London, 1965

Godwin, John, *Occult America*, Doubleday, New York, 1972

Graves, Robert, *The White Goddess*, Noonday Press, New York, 1966

Grivy, Emile Grillot de, *A Pictorial Anthology of Witchcraft, Magic, and Alchemy*, University Books, New Hyde Park, New York, 1950

Guest, Lady Charlotte, *The Mabinogion*, J. M. Dent and Sons, London, 1906

Heinlein, Robert A., *A Stranger in a Strange Land*, Berkeley Books, New York, 1961

Hershman, Florence, *Witchcraft, U.S.A.*, Tower Publisher, New York, 1971

Hill, Douglas, and Williams, Patrick, *The Supernatural*, Signet Books, New York, 1967

Hole, Christina, *Witchcraft in England,* Collier Books, New York, 1969
Holzer, Hans, *The Truth about Witchcraft,* Doubleday, New York, 1969
———, *The New Pagans,* Doubleday, New York, 1972
Huebner, Louise, *Power through Witchcraft,* Nash Publications, Los Angeles, 1969
Huson, Paul, *Mastering Witchcraft,* G. P. Putnam's Sons, New York, 1970
Hughes, Pennethorne, *Witchcraft,* Penguin Books, Baltimore, 1965
Johns, June, *King of the Witches,* Coward-McCann, New York, 1970
King, Francis, *Ritual Magic in England,* Neville Spearman, London, 1970
———, *Sexuality, Magic, and Perversion,* Neville Spearman, London, 1971
Kriss, Marika, *Witchcraft,* Award Books, New York, 1970
LaVey, Anton, *The Satanic Bible,* Avon Books, New York, 1969; University Books, Secaucus, N.J., 1972
———, *The Compleat Witch,* Dodd, Mead, New York, 1971
Lea, Henry Charles, *Materials towards a History of Witchcraft,* University of Pennsylvania, 1939
Leek, Sybil, *Diary of a Witch,* Signet Books, New York, 1968
———, *Complete Art of Witchcraft,* World Publishing Company, New York, 1971
Lefebure, Charles, *Witness to Witchcraft,* Ace Books, New York, 1970
Leland, Charles Godfrey, *Aradia, Gospel of the Witches,* David Nutt, London, 1899; Hero Press, New York, 1971
———, *Gypsy Sorcery and Fortune Telling,* University Books, New Hyde Park, New York, 1962
———, *Etruscan Magic and Occult Remedies,* University Books, New Hyde Park, New York, 1963
———, *The Mystic Will,* Hero Press, New York, 1972
———, *Legends of Florence,* 2 volumes, David Nutt, London, 1895

———, *Memoirs*, 2 volumes, William Heinemann, London, 1893
Lethbridge, T. C., *Witches*, Citadel Press, Secaucus, New Jersey, 1972
Levi, Eliphas, *Transcendental Magic*, Rider and Company, London, 1923
Lyons, Arthur, *The Second Coming: Satanism in America*, Dodd, Mead, New York, 1970
Mallet-Joris, Françoise, *The Witches*, Farrar, Straus and Giroux, New York, 1969
Maple, Eric, *The Dark World of Witches*, A. S. Barnes, New York, 1962
Martello, Leo Louis, *How to Prevent Psychic Blackmail*, Hero Press, New York, 1966
———, *Weird Ways of Witchcraft*, H-C Publishers, New York, 1969
———, *Hidden World of Hypnotism*, H-C Publishers, New York, 1969
———, *Black Magic, Satanism, and Voodoo*, H-C Publishers, New York, 1972
———, *Understanding the Tarot*, H-C Publishers, New York, 1972
———, *Curses in Verses*, Hero Press, New York, 1971
———, ed., *Witchcraft Digest*, #1 & #2, Hero Press, New York, 1972
———, *Witches Liberation and Guide to Covens*, Hero Press, New York, 1972
———, *It's in the Cards*, Key Publishing Company, New York, 1964
———, *It's in the Stars*, Key Publishing Company, New York, 1966
———, *Your Pen Personality*, Hero Press, New York, 1961
———, *1,000 Witchcraft Questions Answered*, Hero Press, New York, 1973
Michelet, Jules, *Satanism and Witchcraft*, Citadel Press, New York, 1939
MacCulloch, J. A., *The Religion of the Ancient Celts*, T. and T. Clark, Edinburgh, 1911

Murray, Margaret A., *Witch Cult in Western Europe*, Oxford University Press, London, 1921
———, *The God of the Witches*, Daimon Press, Essex, England, 1962
Neumann, Erich, *The Great Mother*, Princeton University Press, New Jersey, 1972
Noel, Gerard, ed., *The Pentagram*, issues #1 to #5, London, (August 1964–65. Issues #1, #2, & #3, republished by Dr. Martello, 1972)
Osirus, *Potions and Spells of Witchcraft*, JBT marketing, San Francisco, 1970
Pennell, Elizabeth R., *Charles Godfrey Leland, Biography*, Houghton Mifflin, Boston, 1906
Randolph, Vance, *Ozark Magic and Folklore*, Dover Publishers, New York, 1964
Regardie, Israel, *The Golden Dawn*, Llewellyn Publishers, St. Paul, Minnesota, 1971
Rigaud, Milo, *Secrets of Voodoo*, Pocket Books, New York, 1971
Riggs, Arthur Stanley, *Vistas in Sicily*, Robert M. McBride & Co., New York, 1925
Roberts, Susan, *Witches, U.S.A.*, Dell Books, New York, 1971
Rocco, Sha, *Ancient Sex Worship*, Commonwealth Company, New York, 1904
Russell, J. B., *Witchcraft in the Middle Ages*, Cornell University Press, Ithaca, New York, 1972
Seabrook, William, *Witchcraft: Its Power in the World Today*, Harcourt, Brace and Co., New York, 1940
Shaw, Indries, *The Secret Lore of Magic*, Citadel Press, New York, 1958
Sheba, Lady, *The Book of Shadows*, Llewellyn Publications, St. Paul, Minn. 1971
Somerlott, Robert, "Here, Mr. Splitfoot," Viking Press, New York, 1971
Steiger, Brad, *Sex and Satanism*, Ace Books, New York, 1969
———, *Sex and the Supernatural*, Lancer Books, New York, 1968
———, *Revelation: The Divine Fire*, Prentice-Hall, Englewood Cliffs, New Jersey, 1973

———, *The Resurrection of Manitou,* Doubleday, New York, 1973

Stoddard, John L., *Lectures,* Geo. L. Shuman & Co., Chicago and Boston, 1905

Truzzi, Marcello, *Caldron Cookery,* Meredith Press, New York, 1969

———, *The Occult in America,* Charles Scribner's Sons, New York, 1973

Valiente, Doreen, *Where Witchcraft Lives,* Aquarian Press, London, 1962

Wallace, C. H., *Witchcraft in World Today,* Tandem Books, New York, 1967

Walsh, William S. *Curiosities of Popular Customs,* J. B. Lippincott, Philadelphia, 1907

Wedeck, Harry E., *Treasury of Witchcraft,* Philosophical Library, New York, 1960

Wica Newsletter, Ed. Dr. Leo Louis Martello, Issues #1 to #20, New York, 1970–1973

Wilson, Colin, *The Occult: A History,* Random House, New York, 1971